CIRCUMSTANCES FOR PRAYER

Gene Kobes
Circumstances for prayer

Published by Spines
ISBN: 979-8-89691-229-3

CIRCUMSTANCES FOR PRAYER

GENE KOBES

DEDICATION

I wish to dedicate this book to Christ Jesus, my Lord, and my Savior. You are the one who placed this on my heart: "No greater love has man than this, that he lay down his life for a friend." John 15:13. You did this on the cross for the remission of my sins as well as the multitude of believers. Understanding the depths of this verse provides the framework of servitude, love, devotion, mercy, grace and forgiveness. You are my rock, my shield and deliverer whom I dearly trust in my feeble obedience. I love you Lord Jesus and pray others find you in their hearts in these latter days.

CONTENTS

PURPOSE

I highly suspect when writing a book, one would begin with what purpose it is that this endeavor is coming about. That is because the challenge of writing with cohesion, clarity, organization, and direction is time-consuming. For professional writers, those who write books, newspaper articles, scripts, or plays it comes about as a gift, and natural ability, or a learned vocation.

I have written articles, studies, and sermons with some ease; however, I humbly confess writing a book is another matter. In fact, it has been like a mantel about my shoulders to accomplish. At times, I had wished God would have lifted this mantel from me. What I thought would be months, six at the most, never more than a year has gone on for more than a year now.

I recall my study and military along with work in the defense industry that the standard for writing was something like two pages an hour. That was for technical, or that which were referred to as "White Papers." These were the products we produced both in the German headquarters (Heresamt) and in the Pentagon.

The thought of Circumstances for Prayer was placed in my heart years ago. It was through prayer, circumstance prayer, and circumstance prayer that the purpose for me was God-driven. Proverbs 19:21 comes to mind, "Many are the plans in the mind of a man, but it is the purpose of the Lord that will stand."

In addition to choosing our thoughts and choosing to depend on God's Spirit, we can also choose how we respond to the circumstances of our lives. It would be great if I could state that

I almost always responded with prayer. This was of course not the case. So, at times I confess the circumstance, or circumstances became very serious that the fear of the Lord brought about prayer and change. God can use even painful situations for good. God will develop within us a mature character with the use of the Holy Spirit. This character is likened to the character of Christ in our lives because God knows that the more we become like him the more fulfilled we will be.

God produces the fruit of the Spirit in us by allowing us to encounter situations and people that are in opposition. This is likened to the work of a blacksmith in honing iron in a fire and hammering the metal into the desired design whether it be a horseshoe or a knife.

In the discourse of my life, I turned to prayer because of the light or heavy circumstances I was placed in. My prayers were sometimes long or sometimes short but as I reflect, turning to Christ Jesus for comfort was always a blessing. The outcome, a good share of the time was that of thanksgiving.

I am sharing through this book circumstances that have guided my life through time. Each of us has a story to tell when we see and experience God's hand in the providence of our lives. This understanding gives one a better perspective of world affairs. God's Word is a blueprint of what was, is, and is to come.

INTRODUCTION

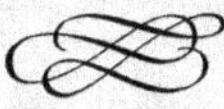

**Give thanks in all *circumstances*; for this is God's will for you
in Christ Jesus.**

1 Thessalonians 5:18 NIV

The thought of *"Circumstances* for Prayer" was originally with
me back in 2005 or 2006, of what God had placed on my heart
then. Our Orange City, Iowa high school class, 50-year reunion
assignment for the 2007 event was to write about our individual
accomplishments through the years. This was when I thought
about how circumstances influenced what I did over the course
of years and how I addressed them by prayer and action. I
submit this take-out from our published journal.

Picture taken from 1957

Class Yearbook for publishing

In 2007 Reunion Journal.

At the time of my ten-page submission to our Reunion Journal, I had no idea God would now have me write a book on the same theme. This is not wishful thinking but as of late, a dominant thought or need for even rest, my God is refreshing the events in my mind like a puzzle for me to fashion into a worthy book for others to use in their spiritual walk with Jesus.

If you grow up in a Christian home one of the first *circumstances* for prayer is bedtime. So, you as a child are praying simple prayers like, "Now I lay me down to sleep, I pray my Lord my soul to keep. If I should die before I wake, I pray my Lord my soul to take. Bless my dad and my mom, my brothers and sister, amen." This is the prayer while you are alone with God. Of course, mealtime prayer by your father was corporate and heard by children. So, the *circumstances* for prayer were common throughout the day and I can attest to the fact that those prayers developed and guided our character in trusting God for our well-being.

In Church, hymns like this buttressed our belief by touching our hearts in solemn episodes of spirituality.

What a Friend we have in Jesus,
All our sins and griefs to bear!
What a privilege to carry
Everything to God in prayer!
O what peace we often forfeit,
O what needless pain we bear,
All because we do not carry
Everything to God in prayer!
Have we trials and temptations?
Is there trouble anywhere?
We should never be discouraged,
Take it to the Lord in prayer.
Can we find a friend so faithful?
Who will all our sorrows share?
Jesus knows our every weakness,
Take it to the Lord in prayer.

Are we weak and heavy-laden,
Cumbered with a load of care?
Precious Savior, still our refuge—
Take it to the Lord in prayer;
Do thy friends despise, forsake thee?
Take it to the Lord in prayer;
In His arms, He'll take and shield thee,
Thou wilt find a solace there.

This 19th-century poem written by Pastor Joseph Scriven in 1865 and placed in lyrics by Charles Converse in 1868 has been one of my favorite hymns. In days gone by, it was more common to sing this hymn, and I miss those days. Our old Psalter hymnal had many songs of praise and exaltation that are not used today. This is sad for they promoted much theology, were easy to remember, and touched the heart with gladness, prayer as well as humble adoration of an all-powerful

God. Hymns are like a Bible of songs that would remain forever, inspired by the Holy Bible. Preachers in the Pentecostal movement, at the close of this age, discovered firebrand youths of which Holy Ghost fire is stoked constantly with zeal and vibrancy. However, the older generation of believers may still be holding the ancient hymns close to their chests. There once was a coming of age when the old masters played musical instruments solo with all the rich ingredients. This is opposed to today's fast rhythmical sequences, like when rappers just cook up hot sounds that go with songs, unmindful of singing parts.

Though time changes everything, hymns remain a medium, linking heavenly devotion with believers in Christ. Nonetheless, spiritual songs come with varieties, some excerpting popular hymns or like hymns, while others seemingly veer into spiritual warfare. They are improvising different voices, tonality, and sounds of which several youths who are true believers find meaning for expression.

The trend away from hymns began decades ago in many churches. Churches do have a need to engage in their culture. The question is whether they are trying to engage the culture towards the worship of the heart of God or to make the house of God engage towards the worship of man's culture. I hope it is the former.

I suspect that back in time, hymn writers spent more time with the Lord thereby integrating theology, than the effort and gifted song writers today. Today, we have many more distractions and media capabilities that facilitate worship. However, for us in an elder age bracket, we do not feel the same heartfelt humble adoration and praise we once had with worship.

If you go to an old church in Europe where architects designed churches with a curved/oval ceiling, you would be able to hear clearly the voice or amplifying instruments. Sometimes there is a special presentation of chant music in a sanctuary designed as such. A description of chant music is that music developed in the 9th and 10th centuries. Gregorian chant is a form of monophonic, unaccompanied sacred song in Latin. The singers would sing as a group and then separate to the balconies on four sides of the sanctuary to sing and respond filling the whole structure with beautiful spiritual sound.

The music from the singers without microphones carries throughout the church like "surround sound." I find it difficult to explain in words the effect of this experience. The only way to replicate the effect of this sound would be to have four speakers in a specially designed room that was acoustically designed.

I believe all Christian worship music is good; however, I am biased as others are for the old hymns of yesteryear.

Let me bear this out in 2010 or thereabouts. Florida State University marching band before the football game played, "Got that Old Time Religion," and the stadium joined in. What a joyous occasion. The crowd of eighty thousand plus may not have known all the verses, but they knew the chorus. This was back in the days of Coach Bobby Bowden and a staff of Christian-believing coaches.

CHILDHOOD

And without faith, it is impossible to please God because anyone who comes to him must believe that he exists, and he rewards those who earnestly seek him.

Hebrews 11:6 NIV

God brings us into *circumstances* to educate our faith because the nature of faith is to make its object real.

Because a child is taught early to pray, he or she responds in prayer to any difficulty he or she may encounter so it then becomes part of his or her character. There is no escape from temptation but when we learn early that God is our shield; It is not only protection, but above all God is comforting.

Have you ever felt vulnerable to a multitude of different dangers? The number of scenarios stacked up against you can be disheartening or perhaps terrifying. This is when anxiety creeps into our lives. Therefore, God gave us His Scriptures; Psalm 3:3 declares, "But You, O Lord, are a shield for me, my glory and the One who lifts up my head."

Sometimes between the 2nd and 4th grade in Christian school, not every day, but often when the curriculum called for it, we were taken to the Lutheran church which was practically next door for prayer time. On the wall of this church situated on a hill skirting downtown Sioux City, Iowa was a large picture of Christ praying in the Garden of Gethsemane. This along with the Bible training we children were receiving, provided a visual rendition of Christ's suffering before the Cross. At the time. I had not yet learned the depth of this prayer in John 17. It was beyond my years but the vision of that picture of Christ praying in Gethsemane was etched on my heart and mind.

Each school day, my father would drive me into the city and I walked the number of blocks up to this school. After school, it was catching the streetcar for the ride home. Sometimes, I would stop at a library just below St. Vincent hospital to listen to story time. As a youngster, we were trusted to manage these commutes. As I remember those times the culture of the rural American was God-fearing and trusting with an abundance of prayer. There was also discipline which involved corporal punishment at home and school.

At school, there was this closet that contained a rubber hose. From time to time, we children could hear weeping coming from that location. I never experienced the effects of that closet, but did I experience the corrective action by the principal while in line at the drinking fountain after noon lunch one winter day?

The *"circumstance"* occurred while we were playing outside when the snow was just right for forming snowballs. That is what we did as kids growing up in Iowa. Well, I made a perfect snowball and launched it at a girl scoring a direct hit. Her response was, "I am going to tell the principal on you." I did not believe her. Snowballing continued until after lunch and school began. While in line at the drinking fountain, the principal stopped by me, and took me by my hair with the statement, "I left word for you to report to me for what you did in the school yard." I don't remember if my feet left the floor from the lifting of my body by my hair, but I was hurting by that action. It was a vivid *circumstance* that is remembered to this day.

It was during this period that we were living in the aftermath of the devastation of WW II and there seemed to be much prayer and thanksgiving. It was a normal ritual on Saturday evening to polish and shine our scuffed-up one pair of shoes to make ready for Sunday services. My concern on Sunday morning was how my father's auto would hold us five children. You see, the wheels on the old REO had wooden spokes. I thought as a young child how could this heavy auto, built like a tank carry seven people with wheels fashioned with wooden spokes?

Activity for young children was mostly outside playing kick the can, playing marbles, or riding bicycles. One may need to Google instructions on kicking the can as well as playing marbles for I do not believe those gaming activities are in the course of a child's play today.

Rainy days consisted of reading, coloring, and playing board games. Obviously, this was before television, but we were not missing anything we did not know about yet.

Of course, Christian school, church, Sunday school, and summer vacation Bible school had me growing in Christ Jesus.

It was in 1948 that our father moved the family to Orange City, Iowa, a small Dutch community in the Northwest corner of Iowa where he had purchased a jewelry store. What is important as my story continues is meeting and making friends with kids from a Gospel (Pentecostal) church two blocks from our home. This led to an invitation to attend their Maranatha vacation Bible school clear out near North Platt, Nebraska.

Vacation Bible school consisted of morning chapel, and afternoon Scripture study, followed by evening chapel. There was no fishing, hiking, or other activities as I reflect. It was all preaching and teaching God's Word. I fell asleep one evening and my friend, Dave Jacobs stirred beside me, stood up, and started leaving the pew. Thinking the service was over, I followed him, only he did not leave the chapel, but went to the front of the alter. Now, I am fully awake and taking stock of where I was with about ten or twelve of us children peering back over the rest of the youth still in their respective pews. At this time, my ears heard the Chaplain say, "These children have dedicated their lives to Christ." My silent prayer or rather thought was, "Lord what did I do?"

Before I continue my story on *circumstances* that led to prayer let me say that I knew I was already saved and had given my life to Christ. My humble understanding of the situation or my perceived CALL meant that I was destined to go into the ministry. This *circumstance* was not Isaiah 6:8, "Here I am Lord, send me." It was simply a surprised acknowledgment of what

God can do. At that time, I was much too young to know of my Spiritual gifts in Ephesians 4:11

GROWING UP IN CHRISTIAN HOME

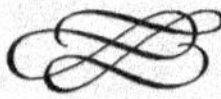

**I am not saying this because I am in need, for I have learned
to be content, whatever the *circumstances*.**

Philippians 4:11 NIV

Orange City, Iowa in 1948 was a quaint small town of around
1,800 souls. In 2013 it became a bustling village of over 6,000.
According to its history, it was founded by settlers from Pella,
Iowa.

In 1870, the settlement was named Orange City in honor of
Dutch royalty. So being Dutch, my father thought it would be a
good fit for the family. There was a Christian school, an old
wooden structure with eight classrooms. Similar, to my school
in Sioux City, it called for rigid behavior, in fact, it was even
more strict in child development.

The culture of the town could bring about thoughts of old-
country Puritanism. The only thing open on Sunday was the
seven or so churches. If you needed gas for your auto, you
better have thought of that on Saturday. I do not believe from

memory that there was even a pharmacy open on Sunday. The conduct of the settlement on Sunday was to observe a day of rest and attend church. The services in our church, the First Christian Reform church were morning, afternoon, and evening. On every other Sunday, the first service was preached in Dutch. My father could understand and speak Dutch, but we children could not for it was not spoken around the house. Six of those churches in town were of the Reformed denomination or theologically aligned with Calvinism. The Gospel church was the exception which has become the Dover Ave. Alliance church.

Before I move on, there was another *circumstance* of snowballing. This time it was an auto that was pulling away from a stop sign. Donny VanWyke and I while walking home from school, each had a snowball at the ready and we launched them both hitting the car. Normally, autos in this case or situation just drove on. This auto came to a sudden stop with the driver getting out ready to give chase. You can only imagine how difficult it was to get away. Open galoshes, lunch pail in one hand, and books in the other caused us to move like two turtles through the snow. I made it to the alley way huffing and puffing and down to a grocery store. I ran through the back door, catching my breath, and peered out the front door. I thought I was clear when just as I was crossing the street there comes that same auto. I started across the city park and made it to the bowling alley below Vogel paint shop.

I knew this well for I set pins there before child labor was illegal. After about thirty minutes I believed all was clear and I walked the eight blocks home. Now, it was about 5:30 or 6:00 p.m. when at the table with my family there was a knock on the door. We were not allowed to leave the table without permission, and it was my father who went to see who it could be. He returned with a stern look and said to me. "It's the sheriff and you are to go with him." Donning my winter coat, I went outside and saw the sheriff's vehicle with Donny in the back seat.

He proceeded to tell the two of us that he was taking us to school where the principal was waiting for us. Our sentence for such a crime was to write on the blackboard 50 or more times, "I will not throw snowballs at autos anymore."

Thinking back on this today one would think we had committed a capital crime and were eligible for reform school. I would like to describe still other characteristics of these school days. They began with prayer. Our teacher would pray very long prayers some lasting 15 or 20 minutes. I likened them to a sermonette. These prayers focused our young minds on learning God's ways. I believe it was in the eighth grade taught by our principal that his opening prayers were not only long but beautiful, I mean, very well-constructed and flowing. While praying he would pace the floor before the class with his eyes open. I humbly mentioned this to my father once by mistake. His response was, "And what were you thinking, obviously with eyes open judging a man in prayer." A good lesson for a young lad.

Here is another lesson on discipline. I was going down the stairs at school while talking with a friend. I prefaced a statement with "Gee Wizz" which was overheard by our principal. This brought about a short lecture on foul or bad language close to cursing. The principal concluded with "be careful how you talk for God is watching." That reminds me of the song, "Be careful little eyes what you see, for the Father up above is looking down in love, so be careful little eyes what you see…"

LIFE IN THE FIFTIES

Together with the details regarding his reign, his power, and the *circumstances* that surrounded him and Israel and all the kingdoms of the countries that surrounded him.

1 Chronicles 29:30 NIV

God did not want Israel to destroy every neighbor nation. Generally, God wanted Israel to be so blessed and strong that other nations would be afraid of attacking it thus recognizing their strength and dominance. One may conclude that this is ringing true in today's world with current events in the middle East.

Life in the Fifties

Historians use the word "boom" to describe a lot of things about the 1950s: the booming economy, the booming suburbs, and most of all the so-called "baby boom." This boom began in 1946 when a record number of babies-3.4 million-were born in the United States. About 4 million babies were born each year during the 1950s. In all, by the time the boom finally tapered off in 1964, there were almost 77 million "baby boomers."

In our home, <u>The Back to God Hour</u> was on the radio every time it was aired. During the 50's the program was already eleven years old. The radio was the internet of its day. Professor Henry Schultze, then soon to be president of Calvin College, began thanking God for the opportunity to broadcast His Word. He began with an introductory prayer in lofty King James English.

"We beseech Thee, O Spirit divine, that Thou will accompany us as we work through the season now begun so that the messages brought today and on the Sundays that follow may cheer and comfort those in sorrow, may sustain and guide those in affliction may strengthen and encourage those that are weakly stumbling along life's pathway, may fill the hearts of the faithful with joy and peace and may move men everywhere to a renewed consciousness of the great glory of our God..." 2

The prayer goes on and on and was likened to the prayers my ears heard at school. I thought then as I do today, if I could pray like that. But then I am reminded, that it is not the lofty prayers by the Bible Pharisees that wish to impress God, but the simple prayers of the humble with a heart close to God

I would like to dwell on a report by Carson Holloway, Visiting Fellow in American Political Thought referencing Alex DE Tocqueville on Christianity and American Democracy. I bring this up to further describe the 1950s which may have provided the last vestiges of Puritanism in the United States. Essentially, Tocqueville was impressed with American Democracy in 1830 when he traced the foundation of our political beliefs on the moral code that was preached from the pulpits each week. He concluded that our democracy would remain strong so long as our church body remained faithful to God. He stated that our democracy would begin to falter when our population begins to become more unchurched, and we lose our moral guidepost.

America's religious landscape has changed markedly since Alexis de Tocqueville visited the United States and wrote <u>Democracy in America.</u> In fact, the rapidity of change or rate of change has markedly increased with each decade. One could NOT say today, as Tocqueville said in the 1830s, that all commerce and activity stops on Sunday that everyone in American public life stops on Sunday, or that everyone is obliged to profess respect for Christian morality. Even civility that goes along with morality seems to have been attacked by a need to promote selfish goals at an immoral cost.

I make reference back to life in Orange City which was considered graciously friendly. When you met anyone on the street or sidewalk it was a good morning, sir, good afternoon, sir or madam, etc. This also entailed tipping your hat or touching the brim with respect. This became part of our character growing up. From memory, respect for elders was a common practice in Sioux County, Iowa.

There was a Christian trust as well. You did not lock your house in those days. Sometimes the sheriff or town police would leave a note on dad's jewelry store, "You forgot to lock the store," and do it for him. Can you just imagine leaving a jewelry store open today?

The dress for the church for men was a suit with a white shirt. Dress for women was modest with a hat and gloves. A hand fan was carried in mom's purse for cooling for that was before air conditioning. We also left our keys in our automobiles in those days.

This reminded me of an interesting story about that. It goes like this. A farmer's wife arrives home from shopping and asks her husband when he put a compass in the car. He responds with, I did not. Well, you just go out there and check she says. The farmer comes back in the house and tells his wife you drove the wrong car home, now I must drive it back into town and retrieve ours as well as apologize to Harry Kobes, my father, for taking his look-alike green 1950 Mercury auto home.

Tulip Festival

The high life in Orange City was the annual three-day Tulip festival held on Thursday through Saturday evening. The Ferris wheel, booths, and festivities were gone by Sunday morning from what I remember. It was Thursday when we children would wear our Dutch costumes to school complete with wooden shoes to be judged and win a ribbon. There was the tradition of scrubbing the street involving men with yoked buckets of water across their shoulders, and women scrubbing with push brooms.

After this, it was the Volksparade.

Pamphlet pictures are from Tulip Festival in May of 2007 during the time of our 50th Year Orange City High (Dutchmen) reunion.

Notes: 3

Later it was the Dutch windmill dance which consisted of young women in costume then. This was quite innocent with the girls weaving, bowing, and then back-to-back swinging their arms like a windmill.

After graduation from 8th grade middle school, most of my class went on to Hull, Iowa Christian school, or Northwestern Academy. About four of us went on to Orange City public school. It was good attending a small high school. This allowed me to participate in sports and I started out in basketball and track. As a sophomore, I also started going out for football. I was just big enough to make the scrub team which were the battered players the first team scrimmaged against. One scrimmage while tackling our star halfback, I was knocked out (unconscienced). I had the experience of smelling salts to bring me around.

I am going back in time now thinking of what it was like in Orange City in the wintertime. There were snowstorms that blew across the prairie land of Iowa and snow would at times drift up to the height of our garage. This made for hefty snow shoveling for my brothers and me. Of course, we would be checking the radio to see if the school was closed for the day. In those days, the school calendar accounted for weather days. Snowplows had all these gravel county roads to clear for school buses to pick up children from farms in our agrarian countryside.

Christmas time had our main street in town adorned with colored lights. I believe it was about two weeks before Christmas we would have St Nickolas come to the city park by sleigh to distribute candy to the children. The timeframe was kept separate from the Spiritual Christmas birth of our Christ child and the secular observance of the season.

The American Reformed church, a block off main street would play Christian hymns from their bell tower during the season as well. The scene and sound were something like right out of a Kincaid Christmas painting.

It was in the early 50s my father had a visit from two ex-Army airmen that he met at the Sioux City Airbase during the war. The two airmen were Jay Van Andel and Rich DeVos. They signed my father up to sell Nutrilite, a natural food supplement. What impressed me at the time was they drove all the way from Michigan in a Jaguar sports coup convertible that was the most spectacular auto this town ever had seen. These two guys later established the Amway Company. My father sold his jewelry store and went into the Amway business and eventually did quite well. I bring this story up because of the Dutch connection as well as the Christian Walk involved with their shared interests. During those days Christian/Spiritual talks and practices were part of the Amway program. One might attribute those practices to the success of Amway.

School social functions were quite innocent. That is, if there was a school dance, we did the bunny hop or Hokey Pokey. Only "old folks" would know what those movements were. There was no intimate touching/embracing or the like. Today, if those dances exist, they are with young children and not high schoolers who would deem them childish.

In high school I was not sufficiently competitive in basketball and dropped that sport and found I could do okay in track, settling into the 880 or half mile. In fact, I placed first in the district in that race and qualified for the state meet in Des Moines. That was a big deal for this small-town kid. The half-mile is the race that places it on the cusp of a run, yet more than a sprint. It is a lonely race dealing with an individual effort without the support of teamwork. The effort you put out is against the clock and other runners so there is time to pray for endurance which I did.

Now, it is football season, and I think it was my senior year that we were playing Primghar, Iowa. Their school had a guy by the name of Mennage on their team who was reported to be the fastest guy in "Siouxland". Anyway, during the game, Merlin Van Roekel, our end-hit Mennage, and the ball just popped in the air for me to catch. I started out for our end zone and prayed, "Oh Lord, let me run." I could hear Mennage closing in behind me and felt his hand brush down my back just as I was crossing the goal. One might say, that was a novel *circumstance* for prayer.

It is important to acknowledge that my life in high school was not all "Goody-Two-Shoes." Details are not necessary, and some might make light of it and note that it was the normal mischief that boys got into.

Graduation from H.S. and working in the forest of Washington was the next employment for me. This was a job I had had in previous summers that started out first in the Yakima Valley. However, with contacts and *circumstances*, I ended up in the mountains along Stevens Pass. Stewart Goslinga, a high school friend, and I were clearing trails along the Snohomish River below Sunset Falls so potential buyers could walk through the underbrush to visit vacation mountain home sites. Stewart left the site early to return to Orange City, Iowa. I continued until the time I was hit by a falling tree. The *circumstance* was that the developer's son was cutting trees by himself and not fore-warning those in the area. At the time, I happened to be in a ravine as the top of a falling tree snapped down striking me in the head and back. This provided a very good early lesson on how God protects those he has a plan for. The Bible says in Psalms 10:7 **the Lord is my strength and my shield; in Him will I trust.** Incidentally, the hospital ward in Everest, Washington consisted of many patients from logging accidents. At that time forest logging was considered one of the most dangerous vocations.

Northwestern Jr. College was my next step in education which led to playing football and the cause of injuries. I had a tendon in my right shoulder torn and played injured for a game with it being taped up. In the last game of the season, my left hand was broken. After it was healed, I had an operation on my right shoulder. I was six weeks in what I called a Frankenstein brace which held my right arm up and forward. My mother had to cut shirts and winter coats to accommodate this contraption. At night, it was sleeping on my back with pillows propping up my elbow or on my stomach with my arm hanging over the edge of the bed. I have not seen braces like this today for such tendon repair. I suspect microsurgery and a sling for a short period of time is the practice today.

Because of my football injuries and recovery, it was most difficult to continue course work and college, so I dropped out. After full recovery and the beginning of summer, it was off to Washington again to work in the forest. I do not recall how long it was that the company I was working for had a downturn in business and released me. My *circumstances* seem to me to be somewhat difficult.

CONCERNS

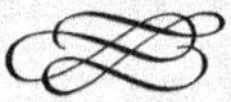

And we know that in all things, God works for the good of those who love him, who have been called according to his purpose.

Romans 8:28 NIV

I was looking for answers to my concerned situation while walking the streets of Portland, Oregon. As I recall, I was praying while looking up and saw this sign, "Join the Army." I went into the office, and signed some papers after a battery of examinations which included a physical. I was concerned that I passed the physical examination because of my right shoulder. Three days later I am on a flight to San Francisco followed by a bus ride to Ft Ord, California for basic training. They called my basic training platoon "Andy's Angels" after Sgt Anderson. He was a tough troop bearing a scar running four inches up the side of his face from an enemy bayonet during the Korean war. There was in effect no nonsense in his platoon for his discipline bore out his character.

After Basic, it was on to Ft. Benjamin Harrison for Finance school. The assignment was not that exciting except that on weekend passes we would bus into Indianapolis for sightseeing outings. After Finance school, seven of our classmates were sent to Fort Hood, Texas, and assigned to the 108th Finance and Disbursing unit. It was about four or six months later that about four of us were levied for assignment to Europe. Military travel in those days was mostly by rail to seaports, then by troop ships to distant ports. For us, it was the seaport of Bremerhaven, Germany, and then rail travel to our respective assignments in France and Germany.

I considered this opportunity with great pleasure for I could not have ever imagined traveling to France. For me, it was an adventurous occasion in which I felt richly blessed. I was assigned to Poitiers.

Poitiers, France

Poitiers

Poitiers, city, capital of Vienne Department of Vienne department, Nouvelle-Aquitaine region is in West-central France, Southwest of Paris. It is situated on high ground at the confluence of the Cain and Boivre rivers. The city commands the so-called Gate of Poitou, a gap 44 miles wide between the mountains of the Loire River and the Massif Central that serves as the connecting link between northern and southern France.

Picture is depicting the Battle of Tours

Poitiers derives its name from the Pictones, or Pitavi, a Gallic tribe that first settled there. t became a Christian center in the 4th century in the time of Bishop St. Hilary of Poitiers. The Visigoths settled there in the 5th century but were driven out in 507 by the Frankish king Clovis. The city became a landmark in 732, when the Frankish ruler Charles Martel (Charlemagne) defeated the Saracens near the city, thus halting their invasion of France. The city and neighboring provinces passed under English rule as the dowry of Eleanor of Aquitaine for her marriage (1152) to Henry Plantagenet (later Henry ll of England). Poitiers was joined to the French crown during the 12th century, but the English won it back at the Battle of Poitiers in 1356. The French reconquered the province and its capital between 1369 and 1374. The French national heroine St. Joan of Arc was interrogated there in 1429.

The city suffered from fighting during the 16th century during the Wars of Religion. After a period of short prosperity in the 16th century, Poitier's economy declined until the 19th century. Parts of the city were destroyed during World War II.

Britannica Quiz

The oldest part of the city has a maze of narrow, hilly streets encircled by boulevards that follow the line of the ancient fortifications. The great artistic wealth of Poitiers is not immediately noticeable, for its many old monuments are dispersed throughout the city. Notre-Dame-la-Grande church above is a good example of Romanesque architecture, with a remarkable 12th-century façade containing a profusion of fine sculptures. The Saint-Pierre cathedral (12th-16th century), built largely in the local Gothic style known a Angevin counts of Anjou and their descendants), has a Crucifixion window that is said to be a gift of Henry II of England.

The carved wooden pews in the choir are among the oldest in France. Nearby stands the 45th-century rectangular Baptistere Saint-Jean, probably the oldest Christian edifice in France. It now houses an archaeological museum containing a collection of tombs dating to the era of the Merovingians (5th-8th century). The Romanesque Saint-Hilaire-le-Grand church was built over the tomb of St. Hilary, the first known bishop of Poitiers, and was restored in the 19th century, the 12th-century ducal palace was incorporated into the 19th- century Hotel De Ville, which houses the museum of Fine Arts that contain a collection of Roman and medieval sculptures. 4

History has always been one of my favorite subjects in school and here I am emersed in preserved old country architectural structures. Weekend passes allowed me to tour the beautiful cathedrals on long walks and breathe the air of history.

Poitiers was the headquarters of Base Section (BASEC) which together with Advance Section (ADSEC) made up (COMZE) Communication Zone Europe. This consisted of several logistic installations backing up the combat divisions in Germany. So, the school system for dependent children was also located here in Poitiers as well. This gave me the opportunity to teach Sunday School.

I also had the opportunity to gain off-duty employment with the casern service club. I believe we had three civilian employees at the club who managed the day-to-day functions seven days a week. Weekend activities included a dance band which was popular. The Army would furnish buses that were sent into Poitiers for free transportation of young ladies to the installation along with free admission to the service club. This included free coffee, soft drinks, and pastry. This was welcomed by us soldiers as well as French citizens in the late 1950s and early 1960s when bicycles were the main source of travel.

Picture of Aboville Caserne

Essentially, the Caserne has not changed much from the time of my stationing there to 2011 when Monique and I visited, for our fiftieth-year anniversary. Out the front gate in the background was a stone stairstep pathway into the city. There were 214 steps down to the base of the hill and across the river before entering Poitiers. Then, after a day of sightseeing, entertainment, and visits to cathedrals; it was 214 stairs back to the Caserne.

While I was stationed there, I had an opportunity to take one vacation to Holland and visit with distant Kobes relatives in

Amsterdam. Facial feature resemblances were noted. I enjoyed the visit to the World Court at the Hague as well as a visit to the Keukenhof gardens. Fields upon fields of tulips made the landscape beautiful for outstanding pictures in multiple colors.

To further occupy my young mind, I was taking a University of Maryland French language course. I believe it was during my second course that I met Jackie who became a regular at the Saturday evening service club dance. We dated once or twice when on one occasion, a *circumstance,* she introduced me to a few of her classmate nursing school friends. One of her friends was Monique Rene Dardillac who was the most attractive of the three girls from the University of Poitiers Nursing School. Life became a beautiful blossom of love, and the fragrance thereof captured my heart. Old fashioned, 'Head over Heels" in love throughout the summer was my blessed *circumstance.* Finally, humbled at heart but courageous in mind, I invited her out for dinner with the intent of asking her to marry me. So, here we were at this fine restaurant, and I could not wait for my anxious heart until dessert. I do not remember what course of the meal we were on, but I pulled out an engagement ring and asked, "Will you marry me?

She had a surprised look on her face and did not answer as I remember. So, my response to her was to keep the engagement ring and think about it. We continued dating without what you consider today, serious intimacy. At this time my belief was that wedding plans were not to be, and we would simply be dating. Well, this particular day, more than a month later, she gets in the auto, my 1953 Studebaker and tells me she has decided. I calmly responded with, "Decided what"? She said I have decided that I would marry you. Now, I am not so calm, and my heart is jumping up and down like a jumping jack as I am trying to drive.

Now, I was scrambling to get the approval of my command and began to complete paperwork for a background check on Monique. Her father was killed during the WWII while fighting in the French underground. So, it was her stepfather who gave the blessing for our marriage. During those years, it was the concern of the U.S. government that there were no communists in Monique's family.

At that time marriage consisted of two ceremonies. One was at the Hotel deVille municipal building in the city. The second ceremony was at the Caserne chapel. France keeps civil and religious ceremonies separate which makes for interesting planning.

PHOTO OF WEDDING

Setting the date of marriage involved a prenuptial understanding. We would be married in my Protestant church (Post Chapel), and Monique being raised as a Catholic, could keep her French citizenship. It was a cold day on the 7th of January 1961. The reason for a winter wedding was that my return to the U.S.

was drawing nigh. Even so, I needed to extend my tour of duty to May, three years from my enlistment date.

The wedding was somewhat unique in that I had the whole ceremony translated and printed into French for Monique's relatives. Lt. Murray our 27th Finance and Disbursing Unit Commander sang the opening wedding march. As the ceremony progressed, Monique was supposed to pray the Lord's Prayer in French while the Chaplain and I were to recite it in English. Well, Monique started in synchronized French and reverted to English mixing up the Chaplain and I in an uncoordinated prayer. The attendees may have been somewhat amused as our Lord God as well. Whatever the *circumstances* were, the Providence of God in our lives has had us together for over sixty- three years as I write.

I have come to understand that two or three or more years in the service of one's country is a very valuable time in one's life that allows young people to pursue personal development. This is before starting college or entering the workforce. According to Paula Fass, PhD, History Professor Emeritus at the University of California at Berkeley, 98% of students who took a gap year between high school and college reported that the deferment helped them develop as people and 97% said it increased their maturity. Gap-year students tend to have GPAs that are .01 to .04 percent higher than their peers.

In the same article, Isabel Sawhill, PhD Senior Fellow in Economics Studies at the Brookings Institution said, " Many young people are floundering today. They are uncertain about what they want to do with their lives. They end up missing a structured opportunity that would allow them to feel needed and capable.

Participants in national service would also gain real-world skills that would help them for the rest of their lives." 5.

This would also add to a healthier appreciation of what our country stands for. Prior national service gives our elected officials a better understanding of our country's defense. Mandatory national service would also foster unity by bringing people from diverse backgrounds together. Dan Glickman, former US Representative (D-KS) stated that mandatory service would be a solution to our current dysfunction because National service, be it in the military, Peace Corps, or other public or private sector offers opportunities throughout the country.

The *circumstances* of my break from college, army training, service, and back in college were measurable by the grades I received in coursework. Before, I humbly submit I was unfocused and struggling with grades. Back in school at the University of Iowa, I was 22, more mature, serious, studying, married, and an honor student. I believe it appropriate here for me to state: Proverbs 16:9 "A man's heart deviseth his way, but the Lord directeth his steps."

BACK IN SCHOOL

Now, when all has been heard; here is the conclusion of the matter (*Circumstances*), Fear God and keep his commandments, for this is the duty of men. For God will bring every deed into judgment, including every hidden thing, whether it is good or evil.

Ecclesiastic 12:13-14 NIV

FAST FORWARD

In College at that time, I explained to Monique that I needed to go on to the seminary to become a minister. I remember my call at Bible camp. "These children have dedicated their lives to Christ." Monique's response was, "I did not marry you to be a pastor's wife, besides I don't even play the piano." This was stated not to make light of it, but really in a more serious tone. There was also discussion about going on to law school. Besides the remaining two years of undergraduate study, law school would entail an additional three years of study. Monique was entirely against this, so after further discussion, it was decided that I would go back into the military by taking ROTC for the last two years of my degree at the University of Iowa. The *circumstances* for all these events to take place are as of late understood. God knows the end from the beginning. In essence, He knows all things. In addition, I joined the Army Reserves in Iowa City for the experience and welcomed income.

Our son, Thierry was born October 29, 1961. What an advent of joy it was with the birth of our son, Thierry Eugene Kobes. It was a glorious day filled with God's blessing. He was baptized as a child in the historic Danforth Chapel on the grounds of the University of Iowa by Reverend Wayne Kobes, son of Uncle John and Aunt Ethel. They were staunch members of the United Methodist Church. In fact, Monique and I attended their church located across the street from the university. I can still remember the pastor, Dr. Dunnington, who would fill the church to the last pew in the balconies with students.

Then, it was the fall of 1963, and lunchtime on campus as I was leaving my part-time job at the Geological Survey. I was heading to the university union for lunch and students were weeping. What is going on I asked. "Don't you know our president has been shot!"

John F. *Kennedy*, the 35th president of the United States, was assassinated on Friday, November 22, 1963, at 12:30 p.m. CST in Dallas, Texas, while riding in an open automobile. 6.

Catholics into the mainstream of American society.

His eloquent inaugural, with Boston's Cardinal Richard Cushing offering the prayer, seemed to fulfill the promise of American Catholic history. He graduated from the University of Notre Dame in 1960 and like many of my generation, I fell in love with John Kennedy. His intelligence, grace, and willingness to confront hard truths (movement on civil rights, resistance to military options during the Cuban missile crisis, his American

University address) and, yes, his "style" especially, for me, at press conferences, drew me in.

I thought then and think now that this experience was deeply religious, as deeply religious for me as any experience "in church." Religion is about what matters, and America really did —and does—matter. Sociologist Robert Bellah famously used President Kennedy's inaugural address to revive consideration of what scholars call "civil religion." The assassination and its aftermath stirred profound feelings that had much to do with the love of God and neighbor as well as love's absence.

So did the 1968 murders and mourning of Bobby Kennedy and Martin Luther King. We were stirred by JFK, then he was murdered. How many young Americans were stirred by Dr. King's "dream," and then they too had to face the dreamer's brutal murder? JFK and MLK mattered, and so did the people and the nation they loved.

There are moments of Catholic life—we call them sacramental —that give us a taste, a sample, of the promise of the "people of God" and "body of Christ." So, there were some moments of national experience that gave us a taste of what Martin Luther King called "the beloved community." Words from such leaders touch our hearts because they relate to our actions. I would suggest that our own feelings at these moments-depression leave us powerless as evil hits us on the head. There exist, however, renewed hope, a sense of solidarity, and shared responsibility as we mourned with our neighbors.

So, what is a genuine religious response to moments when faith is challenged by unspeakable evil? Recently Pope Francis described in words that help us dream again of "one nation under God" as we remember Dallas in November 1963: "The primary task awaiting the church is that of witnessing to the mercy of God and encouraging generous answers of solidarity to open to a future of hope, because where hope grows, energies and commitment are also multiplied for the construction of a social and civil order that is more human and just. Then new potentialities emerge for a sustainable and healthy development."

John Kennedy's life and presidency were tragically shortened. Yet his legacy, formed by a vision that was unmistakably rooted in his faith, had flourished because, beyond his intelligence, grace, and willingness to embrace hard truths, he persevered even in the most troubling of circumstances. He never lost sight of what united our nation and the global community and the inherent hope and solidarity that provided for us all.

There was much prayer during this period as I remember and reverence was in the air. The shock of this *circumstance*, losing our president to an assassination reverberated throughout the nation. 7

RETURN TO MILITARY

For I have sent him to you for this very purpose, that you may know about our *circumstances* and that he may encourage your Hearts.

Col 4:8 NIV

My Reserve Officer Training (ROTC) at the University of Iowa was not that eventful. Since I had prior service, it was only necessary for me to enroll in the advanced program. My junior year was followed by six weeks of summer camp at Fort Riley, Kansas. Prior service did help my camp rating and I was pleasantly surprised that I qualified for flight training. This program was conducted at the Iowa City airport by a contractor during my senior year. The program consisted of 36 hours of ground school and 36 hours of flight school whereby we could qualify for a private pilot license. Flying a P-22 Piper Colt with fabric outer covering in the January-February timeframe was, however, not a cup of tea. Sometimes the aircraft had to be prop-started. The single radio had to be frequency-tuned by tone from navigation to tower frequency. It was rustic flying, to say the least.

From memory, I believe we cadets in the advanced program received about $30.00 a month stipend which was good for the times. My monthly tuition was $35.00 a month and my married student housing in World War ll Quonsets near the stadium was $35.00 a month. My part-time employment at the State Geological Survey on campus brought in another $1.15 an hour. A few of us poor students would also sell blood at Mercy Hospital for $15.00 a pint every six weeks. These figures are provided to indicate how we would survive as students without parental support or student loans. In my case, Monique and I were blessed by her employment at Mercy Hospital as a nurse. Oh, and my Army Reserve pay was another source of income.

As a Distinguished Military Graduate (DMG), I was able to choose my branch of the Army even though it was not difficult to get Infantry during 1965, the beginning of the Vietnam War. My thought was Biblical. John 15:13, "GREATER LOVE HAST NO MAN THAN THIS, THAT HE LAY DOWN HIS LIFE FOR A FRIEND." I do not remember if I quoted it correctly then, but that was on my heart. It was not my "bravado" but simply my deep feeling of trusting my God for keeping me safe and secure.

Infantry Officer's Basic at Fort Benning Georgia was uneventful. It was when I was about to enter Parachute training that I received an urgent letter from my aunt that Monique was having significant problems with her pregnancy. At the time, Monique with our son Thierry, were vacationing in France with relatives. Aunt Ethel and Uncle Johnny were as close to us as parents, so the urgency of her letter was paramount. A phone call with Aunt Ethel relayed the insistence that I take emergency leave and travel to France. Telephone communications with

Monique were not to be for she was with her sister at a beach house on the Ile de Re, (no phone service). The next day with emergency leave approved, I was on a flight to New York with connections to Paris. It was train travel from Paris to Poitiers where Monique's parents lived. My arrival was a surprise to them for they were not aware of any issues with Monique's pregnancy. So, it was the three of us, now by train, to LaRochelle then travel by boat to Il de Re. If I remember this bizarre journey, it was a short walk to Monique's sister's cottage. Now it is Monique who is very surprised to see me.

After an explanation of events, it was backtracking to Poitiers. Then it was by U.S. Army ambulance to a hospital in Tours, France. There we found out that Monique had lost a twin to our daughter Nathalie. Later, I am on my way back to Fort Benning for Parachute training. Monique and our son Thierry were to fly back to Iowa where they would be staying until we all were on our way cross country to Fort Lewis, Washington. I neglected to mention my discomfort in traveling to Washington. You see, I had two sprained knees, three cracked ribs, and a cold. The injuries were from my last parachute jump where my main parachute failed, and I needed to deploy my reserve. Obviously, my landing was not textbook.

I need to mention that Monique was not all that comfortable as well with her pregnancy over the course of our 1,700-mile journey west.

I was assigned to the 4th Infantry Division at Fort Lewis, Washington where we were to train and retain the soldiers of the division before deployment to Vietnam. During this period, one could characterize the training as 'high tempo'. The weekends we did have off were filled with sightseeing trips in the mountains. The space needle in Seattle and the ferry ride across the Puget Sound were fondly remembered. For old-time sake, I did remember a trip to Sunset Falls on the Snohomish River where it was in that area I was injured by a falling tree years ago.

Small and large unit training was accomplished at the Yakima Training grounds. The training area was known for the abundance of rattlesnakes which were somewhat unnerving while sleeping in our tents.

Other events at Fort Lewis were the traditional New Year's Day visit to your Battalion Commander's home. In my case, it was LTC Crizer, 3rd Bn 8th Infantry Bn. His quarters just happened to be those of General Eisenhower when he was an LTC at Ft Lewis in 1909. This information was imprinted on the concrete stairs to the front door.

The other very important event in sequence at Ft Lewis was the birth of our daughter Nathalie, on February 21, 1966, at Madigan Army Hospital. This beautiful *circumstance* blessed Monique and me then with a daughter to balance and fulfill the family. The last remembered event was promotion to 1st Lieutenant. Oh, I should mention that I was selected to attend the Jungle School in Panama. This three-week course helped prepare me for the jungles of Vietnam.

I am eventually assigned as the Executive Officer of C Company, 3rd Battalion 8th Infantry, 1st Brigade, 4th Infantry Division. This position placed me in the advanced party of the Brigade which had us fly to Vietnam. The balance of the Brigade went by ship out of Seattle. The host Battalion for our advanced party was a battalion of the 101st Airborne Division. So, we had the experience of a few small enemy engagements before our troops arrived in the country.

Later, I took over the 4th Platoon which enabled their Platoon leader to take a break. After several battles, I was sent back to

Division Headquarters to run patrols and it was maybe two months later when I heard that my company was hit hard. We lost our Company Commander and one platoon leader besides a number of men, as well as many wounded.

So, I volunteered to return to my platoon since the Platoon Leader who had my platoon was critically wounded. Life in the jungle triple canopy mountainous terrain of Vietnam II Corps was not easy. Normally, we carried three or four days of rations, three or more canteens of water besides four or more M-16 magazines of ammo. This amounted to an average of over 60 to 70 pounds of weight in our ruck-sack. We also had grenades and other equipment like an entrenching tool, M-16, bayonet, and poncho strapped on. Candy bars in old C-rations were okay for energy but tasted like something you would never buy in a store. Take all this equipment, rations, and stuff while struggling up and down the mountainous terrain of II Corps made you brut hardy if you weren't already. The 4th Division was made up initially of men from Alaska, Washington, Oregon, Idaho, and Montana and a significant number of them were lumberjacks, a very hardy experienced group of mountain men. It was after several battles that we began receiving well-trained urban soldier replacements who after a few months in the country muscled up. I say muscled up, instead of bulked up, for movement and activity while the heat of a jungle environment kept us lean. When I left Vietnam in 1967, I weighed 130 pounds in a 5'8" frame.

The jungle streams swarmed with leeches, so one needed to check exposed areas of the body after crossings. At times in the mountainous terrain, it was necessary to prop oneself up against a tree for the night for support. Monsoon rains would fill our fox holes to the top with water and cold elevations of the hills and mountains made for just a miserable existence.

C Company of the 3/8 Battalion experienced many battles and I remember one engagement that was unique. It was the 4th of July 1967 and my platoon members asked if they could fire off some old ammunition in celebration of the 4th. I checked with the company that contacted the battalion. The response was negative, so there would not be any ammunition expenditure celebrating July 4th. Well, sometime before midnight my platoon opened up with live fire. I went forward to emphasize that our requests had been disapproved. The response I received was an excited stuttering report from my riflemen, "Sir, we have contact, and, and one went right by me". Well, I thought 'crapes', I must have passed the enemy going forward, then, I had to be careful retracing my way back to my radio to report. Next, we were sweeping our interior defensive perimeter for enemy presence. Then, this North Vietnamese soldier jumps up before me with a rifle over his head screaming Chu Hoi, Chu Hoi, (I surrender). My, what carnage he could have caused, for his AK-47 still had a banana magazine seeded in the weapon. Our loan prisoner was helicoptered out after we had swept the area. There is a funny side to this engagement. When I located my platoon sergeant, he was naked. His response was, "I could not find my pants and shirt." I had previously instructed him; that you really need to sleep in your jungle fatigues.

There were several other battles before a very large battle called the 'Battle of Three Trees' which occurred South of DuCo, Chapter 20 in the book, "The War of Innocents." By Charles Bracelen Flood. 10

The 3/8th Infantry Battalion, 1st Brigade, 4th Infantry Division was operating along the border of Laos and Cambodia in the central highlands of Vietnam. The whole area was mountainous with double and triple-canopy jungles. This made any movement slow and difficult as well as the difficulty of maintaining any integrity of a diamond formation. This type of formation provided for all-around security. Overnight security was accomplished by an old-fashioned circular array with foxholes dug in case of enemy contact through the night.

Morning consisted of sending out platoon-size patrols to our flanks and toward the direction we were to move the following day. This day, the 2nd platoon encountered the enemy to the South of our company.

There were frantic calls for artillery support from the 2nd platoon before it was overrun. It was not long before the enemy reached my platoon at the company base at three trees. This area was relatively open except for these three trees.

I was shouting at my platoon to execute claymores, a close-in curved mine approximately 15-20 feet in front of our positions. I picked up commo with artillery calling for adjustments. Enemy mortars were coming in then and I was praying that they wouldn't come into our foxholes. I Just had gotten down when my foxhole was raked by automatic weapons fire which also shot off my radio antenna just above the base.

Enemy rockets were coming in and the noise of battle became deafening.

Soon, our airstrikes were coming in and I am wondering why they, the U.S. Airforce were releasing 500 lb. bombs behind our perimeter. It is very disconcerting that their impact would be far enough forward, another cause for a short prayer. "Lord let the bombs impact on the enemy." The reason I looked back was to make sure I was not rising in front of B Company's machine guns of men who had taken up supporting positions behind my platoon. B Company began the day located approximately 600 meters to our North. They had to double-time it to reinforce my platoon. Our 3rd platoon patrol made it back to the company base which bolstered our left flank.

The reason the Air Force bomb runs were coming from behind us from the North forward was that the Battalion did not want to shut off the artillery. The air above the battle became extremely crowded so the effects of combined arms had to be strictly coordinated so the likelihood of friendly casualties would be reduced.

Above the battle, I was screaming at my machine gunner to hold down his rate of fire so as not to burn up his two barrels. Well, he did but bravely went forward to pick up an enemy machine gun on wheels. I do recall an order to my platoon to fix bayonets because close combat was taking place. Our friendly forces and the enemy where were both throwing hand grenades. It was felt at the time that the enemy Regimental commander must have lost control of his units because they continued the attack in the face of overwhelming defensive fire.

The After-Action Report has since been declassified. I found it while searching Google.

Statistics of battle: 4,600 rounds of Artillery were fired in support from 175 mm, 155 mm, and 105 mm howitzers.

A total of 18 Air Force tactical air strikes, and Countless helicopter gunships run using rockets and mini-gun fire.

Later a platoon of tanks arrived as well as reinforcement of A company, so then our whole Battalion with the exception of Delta Company was committed.

Later that evening, a B-52 strike was involved with hitting suspected avenues of enemy retreat. 11

OUTCOME

We lost the 2nd Platoon (20 plus men) which was on patrol directly in the path of enemy advance toward my platoon at company base. Our Battalion also had 41 wounded.

Providence of God

You see, at that morning's briefing, Charlie Barrett 2nd Platoon Leader volunteered for my patrol because he would be the lead platoon the following day in that direction, and he wanted to know the lay of the land. It was to be my platoon patrol mission, so I told Charlie we could both take the patrol with two squads and each leave two squads back at the company base. Charlie stated that he wanted his whole platoon, so the company Commander said settles it, Kobes; You stay back at base. God's providence one may say.

We lost Charlie's whole platoon that day, overrun by a North Vietnamese Regiment. Normally, the strength of an enemy Regiment was 1,500 soldiers. Enemy losses were estimated at over 300 Killed In Action, (KIAs). Of the five major battles the 4th Infantry Division fought, the battle of Three Trees was included as one of them and it was centered on my platoon. To this day, it is difficult to reflect on that battle. The sound and lethality coupled with the visual of all these weapons of war going on about you is a nightmare. You cannot capture in words the complete violence of warfare. The battle lasted the better part of the day.

After B company passed through my platoon to sweep forward of my unit, my unit was tasked to search the remains of many enemies maybe 20 to 30 feet from our foxholes. My heart softened with compassion for I was viewing pictures of children, wives, and families of the fallen enemy. The next day, there was a memorial for the U.S. killed in action, (KIA) of Charlie's 2nd Platoon.

There were more battles before my return to the U.S. Before I leave my ground assignment, I wish to mention here a book by Ivan Pierce author of, "An Infantry Lieutenant's Vietnam." It is a good read and covers more detail of life, battles, and the jungle than I have provided. Why we did not mention each other as members of the same company I do not know. Perhaps the changing of assignments that we both experienced had something to do with it. The epilogue in his book was inaccurately reported to Ivan for I was present during the battle.

A few things that were not mentioned to this point was the presence of 'jungle rot'. This was a tropical ulcer-skin disease caused by constant water emersions. Venous snakes like cobras were also a threat. Once in a firefight, I was behind a gravestone for protection. After the engagement subsided, a member of my platoon cautioned me to be careful moving out for there was a raised cobra on the other side of the gravestone I was behind.

Vintage photo circa 1966 Vietnam during an interview with WHO

While reflecting on the number of battles that I was involved with, I am reminding myself of how many times I trusted God for protection.

TRUSTING IN GOD was the bedrock of my belief for He answered my short prayers in the heat of battle.

What does it mean that God is a shield for us? This historical visual of a shield in battle deflecting the enemy's attack can feel irrelevant to us today. However, there is a shield we can glean context from that is protecting us at this very moment. We only need to lift our gaze, as King David did in Psalms "The heavens declare the glory of God; and the firmament showeth his handi-work. Day unto day uttereth speech and the sky above proclaims His handiwork. Day to day pours out speech, and night unto night reveals his knowledge." Looking to the heavens and sky, we gain insight into God's protective nature. Psalms 19:1-2

We have an advantage King David did not have. We can under-stand more of the heavens' declarations and the sky's speech because of scientific discoveries made since his time. Looking up, we can consider Earth's atmospheric blanket and gain insight into the precise ways in which God is a shield for us. The earth's atmosphere is far more than cosmic coincidence. It is circumstantial. In Genesis 1:2-3, we see God setting the stage for life on earth: "And the Spirit of God was hovering over the face of the waters. And God said, 'Let there be light,' and there was light." Knowing the exact conditions, we would need for Earth to be habitable, He covered our planet with a protective atmosphere — a shield against countless dangers.

With slightly less than 21% oxygen, the earth's atmosphere creates a perfect shelter. If its oxygen level were to rise one percent, the likelihood of wildfires would increase by 70%. Can any of us imagine living on a planet with such an exponential increase in fires? Conversely, if the atmosphere's oxygen level was slightly less, we could not live here. Not only is it the perfect balance of oxygen, but it also guards us against deadly substances. We often think of our atmosphere as the earth's blanket. However, it operates more as a filter, protecting us from harmful radiation while, at the same time, working with our seas to maintain our climate.

Without the scientific advancements of our day, King David could not have grasped any of this as he stared into the heavens. However, what he did know was this; God's creation speaks to His wisdom, providence, and provision. In His foreknowledge, God created a shield for the earth to sustain our lives. But it's not only our physical lives He wants to preserve. No, God Himself is the protector of our souls and watchman of our spirits. As the atmosphere is constantly defending our planet, God guards us in countless ways every day. Just as the atmosphere filters out harmful substances, God deflects toxic thoughts and worries from our minds. He diffuses the fiery attacks of the enemy. On this side of heaven, we'll never realize the full extent of His protection.

Looking at all God has made, including a shield protecting every piece of His handiwork, may we remember how carefully He protects our lives. He is a shield for us. 12

Here are ten verses about God's protection.

1. *"This is God, His way is perfect; the word of the Lord proves true; He is a shield for all those who take refuge in Him."* *Psalms 18:30*
2. *For You bless the righteous, O Lord; You cover him with favor as with a shield".* Psalm 5:12

3. *"And the peace of God, which surpasses all understanding, will guard your hearts and minds in Christ Jesus."* Philippians 4:7

4. *"The Lord is my strength and my shield; in Him my heart trusts, and I am helped; my heart exults, and with my song, I give thanks to Him".* Psalm 28:7

5. Shield For Me from "Hidden in My Heart, Vol IV

6. *"The Lord is my rock and fortress and my deliverer, my God, my rock in Whom I take refuge, my shield and the horn of my salvation, my stronghold".* Psalm 18:2

7. *"He will cover you with His feathers, and under His wings you will find refuge; His faithfulness will be your shield and rampart"* Psalm 91:4

8. *"But the Lord is faithful. He will establish you and guard you against the evil one."* 2 Thessalonians 3:3

9. *"Fear not, for I am with you; be not dismayed, for I am your God; I will strengthen you. I will help you. I will uphold you with My righteous right hand."* Isaiah 41:10

10. *"The Lord will rescue me from every evil deed and bring me safely into His heavenly kingdom."* 2 Timothy 4:18

11. *You are a hiding place for me; You preserve me from trouble; You surround me with shouts of deliverance."* Psalm 32:7

One may also include a shield referenced by Oswald Chambers. 12

"Ye are they which have continued with Me in My temptations." Luke 22:28

It is true that Jesus Christ is with us in our temptations, but are we going with Him in His temptations? Many of us cease to go with Jesus from the moment we have an experience of what He can do. Watch when God shifts your *circumstances*, and see whether you are going with Jesus, or siding with the world, the flesh, and the devil. We wear His badge, but are we going with

Him? "From that time many of His disciples went back and walked no more with Him."

The temptations of Jesus continued throughout His earthly life, and they will continue throughout the life of the Son of God in us. Are we going with Jesus in the life we are living now?

We have the idea that we ought to shield ourselves from some of the things God brings around us. Never! God engineers' *circumstances* and whatever they are like, we have to see that we face them while abiding continually with Him in His temptations, not temptations to us, but temptation to the life of the Son of God in us. The honor of Jesus Christ is at stake in your bodily life. Are we remaining loyal to the Son of God in the things which beset His life in us?

Do we continue to go with Jesus? The way lies through Gethsemane, through the city gate, outside the camp; the way lies alone, and the way lies until there is no trace of a footstep left, only the voice," Follow Me."

In my mind, I do not believe there is anything that equates to the horrors of warfare. Trusting in the Lord Jesus as the great comforter is and has been the solace of fighting men through the ages. Even in rest, the battle environment is a cause for mental and physical stress. Here are a few examples.

I do not know if I was leading a platoon or company executive officer at the time, but a unit was waiting for weather clearance to helicopter some troops out to the Battalion base. One of the troops had seen sufficient combat to cause an obvious mental disorder. He was dancing around a warming fire crying, "The world is a 'Shitpot' and I am in it." After a number of renditions, he took his helmet and heaved it at the Artillery Liaison Officer who was visiting our unit. The helmet struck the officer above the left eye causing a significant gash that would require sutures back at base. I suspect the officer was attempting to reason with the troop which may have caused the aggressive assault. The rigors of warfare that were observed then, remain remembered through life. I speak to this issue for understanding.

Another *circumstance* I remembered as the company exec was when our unit was back at base for rest in the Vicinity of Tuy Hoa. One of the soldiers came excitedly running up to me shouting, "Come quickly, two soldiers were in an argument, and one was holding a weapon aimed at the other." I approached the two with maybe just a few feet between them. One had a M-79 grenade launcher aimed at the other. Without hesitation, I stepped between the two and kept eye contact with the armed soldier. I authoritatively instructed the soldier to lay down his weapon. He complied in seconds. During this short episode, I recalled how important it was then to remain calm with steady eye contact. Consequently, I did not know if he had his finger on the trigger or if the safety was on or off. I also did not know if there was a high explosive round in the chamber or a shotgun round. In either case, whatever was in the chamber would have killed me with the action of a pulled trigger. I do not recall praying in thanksgiving for deliverance, however, trusting in God was my shield. However, I must also emphasize that one does not test our Lord. I also do not consider myself coura-geous, just humbly responding to the *circumstances*.

I was going to pass on to flight school but remembered an unusual set of circumstances while on ground assignment in Vietnam. I was tasked by the Battalion to fly to Saigon and visit with a few of our troops who were in the Long Binh there. While waiting for the return C-130 flight back to Pleiku, I met this French reporter at our air base in Long Binh. So, we were discussing the war in French and she was indicating that she was bound for Tuy Hoa by bus. I told her she may well be captured by the Viet Cong since we did not control Highway 1 traveling North. Her name was Marie France a writer for Paris Match magazine. In a letter to Monique, I described the meeting. In a return response, Monique stated that we should not expect a very good write-up in the magazine, and she was correct. Marie France was captured by the VC and provided a report that was not at all favorable to the U.S. in the French magazine.

AVIATION AND MORE COMBAT

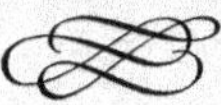

**And we know that all things work together for good to them
that love God.**

Romans 8:28

It is only the loyal soul who believes that God
engineers *circumstances*. If we learn to worship God in
trying *circumstances*, He will alter them in two seconds when He
chooses.

Army Fixed-wing flight training for me began at Ft Stewart,
Georgia in 1967 and consisted of a combination of ground
school and flight. From memory, I believe that segment
consisted of contact flight as well as some instrument training.
The duration of this training was approximately four months.
This training was accomplished using the Army 's T-41 Cessna,
a single-engine aircraft.

Life could be characterized during this time by the significant
movement of the military not only for the one-year tours in
Vietnam but the many temporary assignments for schools and

training.   Our son, Thierry, after residing in France was adjusting from French to English in school with a Southern accent.   I do recall that his transition was remarkedly rapid, really a blessing. Nathalie's first language was French, so she not only had to take on language but also get acquainted with a father she had not seen in a year.

I was going to pass on any event that occurred during flight school but thought then of the humble *circumstance* that occurred with Charlie Finch, a fellow flight school student, and myself. You see, we were two of the I believe five students in our class who had prior flight training in ROTC.   So, we were the first to solo and area solo.   Before taking off this particular day, Charlie gave me a radio frequency we could go to, apart from that authorized that we could use and comment on without being detected.   We took off and flew to the furthest training area where we took turns practicing flight maneuvers.   After a while, we decided we needed to go back to our assigned stage field.   Well, neither one of us had placed the stage field on our maps before taking off from Ft Rucker.   I radioed Charlie, "Do you have any idea where we are in relation to the stage field?" "His response was the only blankety-blank thing I recognize is the cowling of my aircraft."

It was about this time that one of our fellow students on the bus for a follow-on flight with an all-frequency radio picked up our conversation. Next was the voice of the chief instructor pilot, "Students on unauthorized frequency return to correct frequency immediately."   We were instructed to fly back to Ft Rucker using instruments for guidance, then on to the stage field which we both knew from a known point.   We both landed and taxied up to a fuel truck which we both needed.

After we deplaned, Charlie came up to me and said, "The way we got that frequency was by me holding up my fingers for the frequency number". I told Charlie, forget that point Charlie, "Do you realize how close we would need to fly for me to see how many fingers you raised!" We were told to report immediately to Instructor Flight Leader. By the way, Charlie is carrying his parachute. He had dropped his map during our flight and when reaching down, his parachute had popped inside the cockpit which made his flying a bit more difficult. Looking back, it may seem comical today, however, at that time the flight Instructor was so very angry the blood vessels in his neck looked like they were ready to explode. I believe , that if I had not been made Captain that day and the fact that the U.S. desperately needed pilots, we could have been excused from further flight training. As it was, we both received the broken wing award, (not a good thing) at the weekend ceremony. Charlie did me one better by having his parachute deploy in the cockpit.

The next phase of our flight training was at Ft Rucker, Alabama where instrument training was the focus. The aircraft that was used there was the T-42 Beach Baron, a multi-engine aircraft.

During this period, we added to the family with the addition of a cocker spaniel. Church was almost within walking distance. Our neighborhood of mobile homes outside Ft Rucker were practically all military students going through flight training. From memory, there were about one hundred students a month in helicopter training and fifty students a month in fixed-wing training.

At the conclusion of instrument training, it was about a month or more of training in the 0-1 Birddog an observation aircraft. This was the aircraft we would be flying in Vietnam.

Now in Vietnam, I was commanding the 2nd Airplane Recon platoon of Seahorse Company out of Phan Thiet. It was a slow day with little activity until I spotted a Viet Cong (VC) tax point along Hwy 1. I Flew away while seeking fire support or Tac Air. There was nothing available, so I flew back to the area to see if the VC was still there. Without telling me my Vietnamese observer dropped a smoke grenade. Now, the VC knew that I knew where they were. So, I circled around, dove, and punched off two rockets. My rockets were white phosphorous used in marking targets for Air Force fast movers but still lethal to the enemy.

It was then that I observed flashes of rifle fire from the wood line and my cockpit was being shattered with the impact of rounds and shrapnel. Surprising what you do in those seconds besides adding power to pull out of dive, bank, and push to talk. "Catbird 7, this is Seahorse 26, I just received fire, can I get some support now? "Seahorse 26 we are diverting a pair of F4s to your location, can you mark for them". Roger, I am still flyable as I am checking myself and my observer who was scrunched down in the back seat.

I was feeling my body for wounds, gauging from all the holes in my cockpit. My left forearm had Plexiglas fragments from the right-side window that was full of holes. I Did not know at the time I had fragments in my neck as well. I marked for the fast movers (F-4s) and flew back to homefield as I noted that a portion of the leading edge of my right-wing strut was missing as well as a number of holes in my right wing. My Observer wrote me up for the Vietnamese Cross of Gallantry which I received. The enemy action was still ongoing so after getting patched up I got into another aircraft to guide Task-force South of the 101st Airborne Reconnaissance Platoon for insertion into the area. What I was supposed to do, however, was ground myself for 24 hours after being wounded. I explained to my Company Commander later that there were no other pilots readily available at the time to support the 101st.

Later, since the area was a hotbed of enemy activity, we had the Battleship New Jersey on station. I was given a marine gunnery Lt. as an observer to call for fire. It was impressive. Instead of a plumb of smoke and debris from the likes of a 500 lb. bomb, I observed trees being cut down for over 100 meters from the impact of rounds from 16-inch guns. You could actually see the round in the air. I flew a wide birth traffic pattern at the advice of my marine observer. Later, I flew a member of the news media out to the battleship where he photographed the ship firing a broadside, all 16-inch guns together. The ship actually tilts sideways from the effects of a broadside firing.

There was another interesting mission that as of late I failed to include. My unit was tasked to provide an airborne radio relay for a Navy Seal team that was inserted into Cambodia for the purpose of hitting a suspected enemy North Vietnamese prisoner-of-war camp. I assigned six of my pilots' earlier flights taking the last mission myself before turning it over to the Air Force. As I was relieving the pilot before me around midnight 2400 hours, clouds were moving in, and it was becoming more difficult to visually maintain coverage over the area for radio communications. Finally, around 1:00 a.m. (100 hrs) I radioed the Air Force to see if they were ready to relieve me. They have Distance Measuring Equipment (DME). At this time cloud cover had pushed me up to over 8,000 feet. Then, I banked and turned East by compass and prayed to have clear skies ahead for landing. PhanTheit airbase, my home field is located on the coast. Finally, finally, I picked up the lights of fishing boats on the South China Sea and was able to let them down to search for my airfield. There was significant relief from angst when locating the airfield. That was until automatic fire with tracers was coming up at me. What was the enemy doing up at this hour and so close to our airfield? Well, you turned off your navigation lights and entered the traffic pattern for landing.

The point I wish to make from my two combat tours in Vietnam is that the Lord had not only taken care of me, but I did not lose one man Killed in Action (KIA) whether it was in my Infantry Platoon or on my second tour in my Aviation Recon Platoons as well as my Aviation Company. It was like a series of miracles. The Flight Platoon Commander before me and one following me in the 183rd were killed. In the 219th, one of my crew chiefs was bending down to put on his boots when an enemy rocket came through the wall wounding him with shrapnel instead of killing him. An enemy 122mm rocket hit my Birddog ramp in Kontum sending shrapnel through the back of one of my aircraft cockpits and out the front. My crew chief was bending down in the cockpit to unhook the battery which was located just forward of the rudder pedals. Had the *circumstance* for timing not been just right, he could have been seriously wounded or killed.

These combat *circumstances* occurred over the course of three aviation assignments in Vietnam. The first assignment was with the 2nd Platoon, 187th Recon Airplane (Seahorse) Company where I was wounded, followed by reassignment to the 2nd Platoon, 219th(Headhunter) Recon Airplane Company in Kontum. What is important to point out is that the level of combat action in aviation reconnaissance was greater than that of the Infantry because one would fly to the area of enemy engagements to affect the full combat capability of our friendly forces.

The impact of your mission was greater as well. Let me explain this in more detail. I was on night readiness duty when a call came in for support of an engagement about forty kilometers North along the coast. As soon as I arrive in the area, I receive a call from the U.S. advisor with a South Vietnamese unit. He gave me his coordinates, the displacement of the unit, and the direction of the enemy enemy forces. Because of fuel and available time on station, I directed the friendly helicopter gunships in first. An Air Force C-130 gunship, (Spookie) was dropping flares to assist visual placement of munitions. Then I had the 130's begin their gun runs after confirming direction and coordinates with the U.S ground unit advisor. Spookie has mini Gatling guns mounted on the side of their aircraft capable of placing a round in every square foot of an equivalent football field within a few seconds. The visual of this is likened to a tongue of fire reaching down to earth with just every fifth round being a tracer which provides the light of the burst. After this, I called for artillery concluding with "fire for effect". This call is for all artillery guns of the battery to conclude firing at the same time. I do not remember how much time while flying back to home base I began weeping and acknowledging that it was not me but the Holy Spirit who was directing me in my instructions for all the munitions that were expended without the incident of friendly casualties. In prayer, I am thanking God for His guidance, comfort, and support. My, how great is our God.

During daylight combat conditions I can attest to the fact that *circumstances* and tempo of battle can become almost overwhelmingly complicated. This is furthermore significantly delicate at night.

An example of daytime operations follows. I was flying recon North of Kontum in the vicinity of Dak To at the base of the Ashau Valley. There was a call for support by the mix of U.S. and South Vietnamese at DakTo. I called for artillery support from a firebase in the area. Things quickly developed into a full-scale engagement. Enemy artillery from across the border in Laos began marking our U.S. artillery base for which I advised them to expect incoming. At the time I was advised of a long-range friendly patrol that was working just to East of Dak To as well. They mirrored me for confirmation. To be mirrored is for a unit to use sunlight and reflect it toward you. At this time, I thought, my goodness, the puffs of enemy mortars are in the same proximity and right below me.

Then, I observed enemy tanks and armored personnel carriers descending from across the border. Things became even more complicated as I was directing artillery on multiple targets. I started getting intermittent tones on my radio which meant I was being tracked by enemy anti-air radar associated with 37mm guns. So, I had to continually vary altitude and direction so as not to be acquired while directing combined arms fire. Finally, low on fuel, I contacted Air Force tactical fighters and I was turning the battle over to one of my platoon members to return to base for refueling.

I think it only right to include a flight mission which may have seemed tame in comparison to everything else that was going on in Kontum Province. I was to fly an Army troop from Kontum to Pleiku, U.S. Air Base for the purpose of his emergency leave. It was about a 30-minute flight and the tower at Pleiku had me taxied right up to a waiting C-130 for my passenger to deplane and board the C-130. My, how the U.S. takes care of our uniformed personnel. Anyway, I taxied back to the active runway for takeoff back to my home base in Kontum. In reflection, I should have spent the night in Pleiku or flown over to Camp Holloway 10 minutes away. I say this because it was getting dark and Kontum did not have any runway lights. They did have a portable GCA (Glide Control Approach) which when utilized gives the pilot the appropriate glide path to the runway.

I radioed ahead and stated that I would need that since it was dark then. I entered the downwind leg toward the Kontum city lights, turned base while descending, and then final approach as I was picked up by GCA instrumentation. When I turned on my landing lights, I found I was over the bunkers and not the landing strip. The runway was not long enough to correct so I initiated a go-around climbing back to a pattern altitude of 1000 feet. The portable GCA did not offer left or right corrections. The next thing to occur was that I experienced a partial engine failure. My slightly excited call to the tower was MAYDAY, MAYDAY partial engine failure. The tower operator's call back, "Do you want me to shoot a flare?" Affirmative, I answered. Then, I was over Kontum City with full power, yet descending with a somewhat sick feeling. The good news was as I turned on the final approach, I had the airfield in sight and just made the runway before running out of necessary airspace before touchdown. "Thank you, Lord, for you are the one who knows the end from the beginning. You Lord, had protected me yet once again." I prayed.

Another unusual circumstance took place when I was about to take off with a photographer for the purpose of filming the Ho Chi Ming trail in Cambodia and Laos. We had just received radio communications that the code name 'Starlight' was being executed. This code represented the release of a German nurse who had been captured by the North Vietnamese. Before her capture, she was a volunteer at a Vietnamese orphanage. I had the approximate coordinates to fly to and upon arrival, I observed a Mountainaurd group escorting this Caucasian woman along a mountain trail. After a low-level pass, I guided the helicopter to the location for pick-up. It was big news in the press at that time. The original article appeared in the New York Times, September 10, 1973. Monica Schwinn of Lebach, Germany was held captive for four years. She related that two other nurses had died of starvation. Her captivity consisted of marching 62 miles into North Vietnam as well as being beaten to unconsciousness a number of times.

Up to this point, I had neglected to mention my mission as 2nd Platoon Commander, 219th Aviation Recon. Company. Half of my platoon was in support of activity within Kontum Province. The other half of the three aircraft and pilots flew in support of the Command-and-Control Center, the tri-border area of Cambodia, Laos and Vietnam. These 0-1 birddogs were painted black. The pilots wore black flight suits and carried no identifying documents or tags. Their mission was secret at that time for their area of operation was not officially recognized. From time to time these aircraft returned to base at Kontum with holes in the fuselage and once with a major portion of its tail blown off by enemy 37 mm anti-air munitions. My final assignment in Vietnam was commander, the Headquarters Company, 52nd Combat Aviation Battalion (Flying Dragons).

My reflections on the Vietnam War must include a small background before the U.S. became involved and address how we got there.

The two Vietnams (1954–65)

Until 1960 the United States had supported the Saigon regime and its army only with military equipment, financial aid, and, as permitted by the Geneva Accords, 700 advisers for training the army. The number of advisers had increased to 17,000 by the end of 1963, and they were joined by an increasing number of American helicopter pilots. All this assistance, however, proved insufficient to halt the advance of the Viet Cong, and in February 1965 U.S. President, Lyndon Johnson ordered the bombing of North Vietnam, hoping to prevent further infiltration of arms and troops into the south. Four weeks after the bombing began, the United States started sending troops into the South. By July the number of U.S. troops had reached 75,000; it continued to climb until it stood at more than

500,000 early in 1968. Fighting beside the Americans were some 600,000 regular South Vietnamese troops and regional and self-defense forces, as well as smaller contingents from South Korea, Thailand, Australia, and New Zealand.13

From my experience, a large segment of the 1 million North Vietnamese that moved to South Vietnam were Christian and fishermen by trade. Consequently, they lived in seacoast villages. It was these villages that were the focus of attacks by the Viet Cong and North Vietnamese.

I come to understand therefore, the purpose of the U.S. involvement in Vietnam was that of "Just Cause" by stopping the spread of communism in South Vietnam.

Although St. Augustine provided comments on the morality of war from the Christian perspective (railing against the love of violence that war can engender) as did several Arabic commentators in the intellectual flourishing from the 9th to 12th centuries, the most systematic exposition of the Western tradition and one that still attracts attention was outlined by Saint Thomas Aquinas ibn 13thcentury. In the Summa Theologicae, Aquinas presents the general outline of what becomes the traditional just war theory as discussed in modern universities. He discusses not only the justification of war but also the kinds of activity that are permissible (for a Christian) in war. 14

What Were the Paris Peace Accords of 1973?

The **1973 Paris Peace Accords** constituted the agreement that ended the United States' involvement in the Vietnam War. The accords were signed on January 27th, 1973, in Paris, France. Representatives of the US, the Democratic Republic of Vietnam (North Vietnam), the Republic of Vietnam (South Vietnam), and the Republic of South Vietnam (PRG) signed the accords. The PRG represented the communists in South Vietnam.

The Paris Peace Accords defined the parameters under which peace could be achieved and the Vietnam War could be ended. The accords stated that all American troops had to leave Vietnam. The accords were also intended to allow North and South Vietnam time to negotiate a power-sharing agreement and end the civil war that had raged between the two for the preceding thirty years. Finally, the accords provided for a prisoner exchange and withdrawal of troops from Cambodia and Laos, among other points. 15

FAMILY LIFE

Many are the plans in a person's heart, but it is the Lord's purpose that prevails.

Proverbs 19:21

Love bears all things, looking for the best, remaining steadfast during difficult times, circumstances without weakening.

1 Cor 13:7

It is important here to bring the family up to date during my two years in combat. In case of sad *circumstances,* Monique and two children, Thierry our son, and Nathalie our daughter departed for France to be close to her family during my first tour in the Infantry. Correspondence during the Vietnam conflict remained with slow mail. So, our love for each other was by treasured letters that were kept and reread. Time of writing and final receipt was on average three or more weeks for the mail had to travel halfway around the world. Our son started school in France at the age of four. This was the normal age for French children to begin learning in a classroom. For Thierry, it was learning French as well. Likewise, for our daughter who began to talk, it was French.

It is interesting how Thierry explained who he was and where his father was. When he stated that his father was in Vietnam fighting Communists, his classmates responded with, "France is no longer in Vietnam." Then there was a discussion that followed about what nationality was he. He would respond with, "I am half French and a big half American."

It was during my second tour In Viet Nam that Monique and I met in Hawaii for my Rest and Recuperation (R & R). This was a super five days at the Moana Hotel in a seaside room over-looking the beach and ocean. Of note, they were filming <u>Tora, Tora, Tora</u> while we were there. What a coincidence to leave one area of combat in 1968, just to view the history of another being filmed. I do not count this random, but do not under-stand the *circumstance* of why. We saw the Don Ho show which we enjoyed. Do not remember much else except joining up with Bill Berg and his wife. We had been friends through our Infantry combat time in Vietnam, then flight school followed by assignment to the same aviation company but different flight platoons in Vietnam.

My next assignment after returning to the United States was to attend the Infantry Officer's Career Course at Fort Benning, Georgia. Monique and I met in Chicago, Ill. Monique and her children had just returned from France. After purchasing an auto in Chicago, we drove to Iowa to pick up the kids. The children were residing with Uncle Johnny and Aunt Ethel. It was great, a great reunion.

We had our mobile home moved from Fort Rucker to Fort Ft Mitchel, Ala across from Ft Benning. I only bring this up to explain the multiple transitions the children went through because of the many temporary duty assignments (TDY) I experienced. I believe that it was a matter of life then during an extended war. Our son Thierry attended in the neighborhood of twenty-one schools growing up, three of which were during high school. Our daughter Nathalie was not far behind but more stabilized with her last years of high school graduating from Bonn, Germany H.S., a State Department school.

While at Fort Benning, Georgia, Monique studied for the reciprocity of her French nursing license and went back to work to help repay the many airline tickets we had charged for her and her children's travels. Over time this came to be a rich financial blessing to keep the family solvent.

Sometime during the Career course, I telephoned the Infantry branch in Washington DC to see if I might be assigned to Europe for my follow-on duty station. Well, who should I be talking with but Col. Cosby, one of my instructors at the University of Iowa? What a coincidence, one might say but I find it a pleasant *circumstance*. He stated to me that branch had me going to Tallahassee, Florida to teach ROTC at Florida State University. I stated I really had my heart set on a European assignment. Col. Cosby told me to check out an aircraft, fly down to Tallahassee, and affirm my liking or disliking the assignment with the senior (PMS) Professor of Military Science, then get back to him.

I became convinced at the time it was a wise choice, then I had to convince Monique how important it was for my career. This assignment entailed a follow-on course for those of us in class heading to an ROTC assignment. One might consider teaching ROTC a plum military assignment and in reflection, it was during the continuation of the Vietnam war. Qualifications at that time were possessing a college degree and having a minimum of one year tour in Vietnam for which I had two. The downside of the assignment was putting up with war dissent on campus. Looking back, it was not as bad in the south as it was up north on campuses. However, we did have our ROTC classrooms taken over by students on a couple of occasions, but there were no violent activities. It was my belief that FSU President Stanley Marshall in coordination with campus police as well as with our (PMS) Professor of Military Science, Colonel Walter Fraunheim that together they handled disorder extremely well.

At the time of this assignment 1970-1973, I came to believe then it was my leadership that brought about the good fortune in my duties. In reflection, I have come to understand that it was my God who provided me with the ability and *circumstances* of the many outcomes. As the ranking Colonel in ROTC among 53 university programs in the Southeast U.S., Col Fraunheim was to be camp Deputy Commander for ROTC summer camp. He chose me, a lowly Captain to oversee operations in organizing and planning the ROTC camp at Fort Bragg, one of three camps nationwide. Col. Shea Meyer, (Gen. Promotable,) was the Commander. At the time, he was Deputy Commander of the 82nd Airborne Division. The experience I came into was valuable in the furtherance of my career along with the special reports I received.

During my tour in ROTC, FSU was chosen to be one of ten test universities to accept women into the Army ROTC program. The Air Force was ahead of the Army on this issue. Anyway, I had some twelve to eighteen women in my freshman class. It was a big deal for Gen. Bailey, Commander of the (WAC) Women's Army Corps at that time to land on campus by helicopter for the express purpose of speaking to my cadets. I was excused from that class. This timeframe of course was before the integration of women into all branches of the Army. We also had cross-enrollment agreements with Tallahassee Community College and North Florida Junior College in Madison, Florida. So, I ended up teaching on three campuses as well.

I do not wish to dwell on this segment of my military career but do want to explain what God had placed on my heart to write. At that time, I believed it was my bravado and leadership that brought about success when in actuality it was the mercy and grace of our Lord. You see, during that assignment, I was injured once when on a weekend exercise with my cadets. I was running through the woods at night when a pine needle cut my right eye. A fungal infection ensued requiring ten days at Martin Army Hospital at Fort Benning, Georgia followed by an operation. Recovery was painful and seemingly long.

I come to reflect, that it was the *circumstance* that God brought about to get my attention and for this day to remember that although I was a believer, attending Gray Memorial Church within walking distance from our residence, I was not living a true Biblical life.

Another injury occurred when I was required to fly to maintain flight requirements during that period while still teaching ROTC. I would drive to Fort Rucker to check out an aircraft to fly a minimum amount of time every three months. On this particular occasion, I was reaching over the aircraft wheel strut to yank the two parachutes up to put into the aircraft. Something snapped in my back and I thought wow, this is not good. In pain, I took off for Auburn, Alabama to pick up a co-pilot. The weekend was pain, pain, and more pain. The short side of the story was that I was placed in traction at Tallahassee Municipal Hospital for ten days as well as fitted for a back brace. Was this not enough to get my attention, Lord?

Apparently, it was not, for there were more anxious minutes at Fort Bragg with the cadets. While there I saw the opportunity to get some flight time and I checked out a T-41. There was a write-up in the log book that the RMI (Radio Magnetic Indicator) was non-functioning. I thought, no problem, I had the compass backup available for (VFR) Visual Flight Rules flying. I took off and flew for a while and thought, why not get some nighttime in which was another requirement. Well, it was beginning to get dark, and I turned my instrument lights on but the light in the compass was not functioning. No problem I thought, for I would just replace the bulb from my vacuum gauge which I did not really need. Then, I was surprised with the results. All my instrument lights shorted out along with shorting out my radios. Fortunately, I was not that far from Fort Bragg, and upon arrival, I executed a no-radio approach. This constitutes flying a low pass down the lighted runway in front of the tower and dipping your wings while executing a go-around. Then you begin your descent and look to the tower for a green light for clearance to land. In this case, I was relying on the sense of descent and airspeed since I did not have lighted instruments to check the rate of descent, altitude, and airspeed.

Perhaps it is important here to address happenstance. According to Webster: "Happenstances are coincidences, random occurrences, accidents, incidents, events, experiences, occasions".

When you search Scripture, there are over fifty references to *circumstances* which seems to portray a more complex series of steps to arrive at an outcome. They are not random acts, but God directed steps to bring about a desired outcome for believers, nations, and people.

An example that can be used here is one from 1 Samuel 3:15. God never speaks to us in startling ways, but in ways that are easy to misunderstand, and we say, "I wonder if that was God's voice?" Isaiah said that the Lord spoke to him with a strong hand, that is by the pressure of *circumstances*. Nothing touches our lives, but it is God Himself speaking. Do we discern His hand or only a mere occurrence? We must get into the habit of saying, "Speak, Lord," and life will become a romance. Every time *circumstances* press, say, Speak Lord" your servant is listening. We should and must recall a time when God did Speake to us.

As we listen, our ears become more acute, and like Jesus, we shall hear God all the time. Praise be unto You, dear God Almighty.

"There is only one thing you can consecrate to God, and that is the right to yourself (Romans 12:1). If you give God your right to yourself, He will make a holy experiment out of you. God's experiments always succeed. The one mark of a saint is the moral originality that springs from the abandonment to Jesus Christ. In the life of a saint, there is this amazing wellspring of original life all the time the Spirit of God is a well of water springing up perennially fresh. The saint then realizes that it Is God Who engineer *circumstances. 16*

BACK TO EUROPE

Once these signs are fulfilled. Do whatever your hand finds to do, for God is with you.

1 Samuel 10:7 NIV

(signs or circumstances)

While teaching ROTC at Florida State University I also enrolled in a master's program and completed the course work for an MS degree in Education. There was at that time, some thought about going on toward a PhD and leaving the army. However, the excitement of returning to Europe was the more appealing.

Finally, I had orders for assignment to Europe with temporary duty en route at Fort Rucker, Alabama for a transition course to rotary wing qualification. I was assigned as Executive Officer of the 8th Division Aviation Detachment at Bad Kruznach, Germany.

At the time I believed it to be a blessing although Monique came to love Tallahassee and her position at Archbald Hospital in Thomasville, Georgia. A short commute north. I thought she would be happy and the children excited with an adventure at heart. However, the children were settled and content in school there in Tallahassee and happy. Alas, I preceded the family to Germany, and Monique was left to manage the shipment of household goods. I do not remember why the military planned it that way. Perhaps because the U.S. was still involved with a war in Vietnam, and things occurred with more upheaval than *circumstance.* Military quarters were not readily available, so we lived in a small village outside Bad Kreuznach. It was a drafty second-story apartment with oil heaters in each room. It was late fall and cold. The children had to get up early and be ready for busing to the base for school. Monique's auto had not arrived yet and she was left alone in a cold surrounding. In reflection, my heart pinned for her discomfort.

It was not long before her grandmother passed so we traveled to France for the funeral. The atmosphere seemed to be one of depression at the time.

There was a significant change when her auto arrived in the country, and we obtained quarters on base. Monique also gained employment at the small military clinic there. The on-call doctor on the night shift was not always readily available so Monique on occasion played the part of mid-wife in delivering newborns.

There was one serious mission on this assignment for which I considered at the time dire *circumstances.* That was when the weather may have begun under somewhat normal conditions but worsened as the mission progressed. I was on night duty call when a mission was requested to fly two passengers from the Signal Battalion along with six radios to Sembach U.S. Airforce Base. There was a U.S./German exercise going on and the need arose for more radios. The winter weather was marginal, however; for exercise purposes, we were able to reduce visual distance and altitude minimums. Chief Warrant Officer (CWO) Buchannan and I took off around midnight for the approximately 20-minute flight south. Even at night, you were able to distinguish between clear skis and clouds under Visual Flight Rules (VFR). Well, Mr. Buchannan, our unit instrument flight Instructor Pilot (IP) instead of averting the clouds punched into the clouds and called air traffic control for a vector to Sembach. We were now at around 6,000 feet altitude and what you call inadvertent Instrument Flight Rules (IFR). The OH-58 was not designed for instrument flying let alone severe weather conditions. Even though Buchanan was a well-qualified instrument IP I would have preferred to scrub the flight before becoming inadvertent IFR.

For a few minutes, we are fine being picked up by air traffic control and being vectored but, mind you we began to experience icing and the ability to maintain altitude. When air traffic control radioed descend and maintain 4,500 ft, I radioed back that we are passing through. It was not long before traffic control radioed descend and maintain 3,500 ft. We happened to be passing through. Approach control at Sembach then gave us corrections to align us for the runway and gave us descent instructions for an unpublished back course Instrument Flight System (ILS) approach. The reason we were previously unable to maintain altitude was that we were being iced at an alarming rate. Our torque meter which went into the yellow continued to go past med-point toward red. Not a good indication to remain safe and flyable. Even in final descent, we were not able to pick up the runway lights. Our windscreen was completely iced over as we touched down. We had to hover sideways to get off the active runway to the ramp. As we were shutting down on the ramp, I do not know if it was I or CWO Buchanan who called approach control with a big relief and a thank you. After shutting down, I believed I prayed thanking God for yet another time for deliverance. When you look at the terrain around Sembach, it is all hills and mountains. Sembach is the only stretch of flat terrain.

An uptick from flying was that I came out on the major's list and was promoted to 0-4 Major along with receiving my senior wings (1500 hrs. of flight) in the same ceremony. My follow-on assignment was to become the S-4, Logistics Officer of the 1st Brigade 8th Infantry Division located in Mainz, Germany. Aviation had not become a branch by itself yet, so one had to maintain qualifications in a specialty as well as being current in their branch of the Army. There was a period of angst at that time for the Army was going through a Reduction-In-Force (RIF) so the selection rate to major hovered around fifty percent, not good for those desiring a full twenty or thirty-year career.

Operational readiness of U.S. European assigned Divisions required a steady state of qualifications necessitating exercises at several installations like Baumholder, Villesech, and Graffenweir. For the 8th Division, it also required practicing Rhine River crossings from time to time, not a small endeavor. Partial uploading of ammunition was also a major exercise. All these exercises along with Reenforce Europe (REFORGER) made for long days and sometimes non-free weekends.

An upside of my duties was being named a liaison officer to the French Brigade in Trier, Germany. This amounted to an exchange of tactical military experiences as well as social events such as a military ball. Reflecting on that occasion it was humbling to admit the French military band outshined the U.S. in a ceremony, pomp, and musical arrangements. On one occasion the French military performed a 16th century minuet in all its dress and regalia.

After a period of time, I was assigned down to a Battalion, 2nd of the 87th Mechanized Infantry as the S-3 Operations Officer and then later as the Battalion Executive Officer. This amounted to even more time in the field. I remember a time in the dead of winter at Vilseck, when we were in blizzard conditions. Our four-wheel drive jeep was even having difficulty traversing deep snow. Keep in mind this was also before the age of the (GPS) Global Positioning System. We were using good old-fashioned compasses which were hard to read at night in those conditions. It was so cold that my map's transparent overlays were simply breaking up in pieces. That night in what I thought would be a cozy warm billet was cold and breezy. Even in my army sleeping bag, I was cold. Come to find out, my Battalion Commander who I was sharing the room with was in two sleeping bags with the windows wide open. LTC Dickenson's response the next morning was, "I love fresh air."

It is time now to bring the family up to date. Monique was working as a nurse at Wiesbaden military hospital and the children were happy in school. It was about this timeframe I telephoned the branch to see what they had in store for my next assignment. I then learned the Supreme Atlantic Command Europe (SACEUR) was looking for a new commander for the 357th Flight Detachment, the unit that supported General Alexander Haig. Well, what an opportunity I thought. I submitted my application, and short bio and was flown to Mons, Belgium for an interview with BG Dyke chief of Staff. To my surprise, I was selected.

So, we got packed up for yet another European move this time from Germany to Belgium. All the in-laws thought it was great as well for it facilitated theater visits. The children became right at home in the dependent school which had an international flavor of students attending from (NATO) North Atlantic Treaty Organization nations. Their second language French fits right in. It was not long before Monique got on-board at the military hospital in Mons. Monique said it was more like a large Clinic.

I needed to get current with flying again which required more IFR flying. Belgium is not blessed with sunny clear weather. In fact, their auto routes are lighted to facilitate driving. Our UH-1 helicopters were fitted with auxiliary fuel tanks for extended flights. They also had additional instrumentation (DME) Distance Measuring Equipment. Morning and evening fog was normal weather for Belgium.

It is important to mention our respective auto accidents during this period. Monique's Karman Ghia was totaled in Germany and my BMW was totaled in Belgium. In both cases neither one of us was at fault nor were we seriously injured. In both *circumstances*, God's guardian angels were with us.

Life in Mons and Heresies Belgium was one of bliss and tranquility. Mons was the site of (SHAPE) Supreme Headquarters Allied Powers Europe and Heresies was where we found a splendid home to rent across the street from a cathedral. Then, it was waking up to church bells on Sunday, however we attended the Chapel on base that had Anglican services. Even our cocker spaniel enjoyed Heresies for the meat market in the village would give him a bone on his visits.

Because of our extended time in Europe, I took advantage of the non-resident Command and General Staff Course being taught there. Classmates were multi-national which made for an enlightening experience; likewise, in school for the children, Thierry and Nathalie it was interesting. Thierry was correcting the French teacher too often and was excused from class. This was a nice way to put it. By this time, he had also become an accomplished tennis player. When General Haig wanted a good work out on the tennis courts, he would request a good high schooler and the coach provided our son Thierry. So, besides playing fullback in football, he was staring in tennis. I also need to mention that he received a 50cc Honda Motorcycle for his 16th birthday. His fame grew beyond his years, but he still needed dad to drive him and date to high school dances.

I should mention here Christmas greetings at General Haig's chateau was in dress uniform. The formal affair included all his commanders and staff. So, even my lowly position as commander of the general's flight detachment got me and Monique an invitation. Flights for passengers that were coded were interesting as well. Code one was for heads of state, code two for Congressmen and Senators, etc. Flights to London were unique because of the flight pattern we flew. We were required to fly the course of the Thames River, over Westminster bridge to Battersy Towers dock helipad across the river from parliament. The level of your instrument qualification was part of the clearance for your approved flight plan.

There was a significant amount of instrument training because of weather conditions in northern Europe. I recall a time when coming back from southern Germany en route to Mons, Belgium where air traffic control put us up to 10,000 feet. At this altitude and strong winds, our ground speed was a mere 50 knots. So, even with auxiliary fuel tanks we needed to refuel. Air traffic control had put us in a holding pattern in the vicinity of Bitburg. Then Bitburg tower gave us clearance to land cross field to the apron as a flight of F-16s on fuel emergency were landing on an active runway.

During the course of an Army career, I can fondly chalk this assignment up as a real choice blessing. There would be another however, following a stint at Fort Rucker, Alabama followed by German language training at the Defense Language Institute in Monterey, California. This would be a promotion to

0-5, Lt Colonel and the assignment as the Training Liaison Officer to the German (Heeresamt,) Army Headquarters in Cologne. This headquarters was somewhat comparable to our U.S. Pentagon.

In fact, one of the papers, I researched and wrote was describing the likes and differences of our respective commands.

Monique and I had Embassy quarters in Bonn which was then the capital of West Germany. German military life at this level included many military formal affairs celebrating different events. The State Department amenities included a club, pool, tennis courts, movie theatre, and Chapel. The Chaplain was of the Reformed Christian Church. I was still somewhat familiar with Calvinism since I grew up with that doctrine. Life was serene in this community, and it was often referred to as a cozy "Little America." The American presence in Bonn at the height of the cold war was significant. When the wall separating East and West Germany came down, plans to move the embassy to Berlin were put into effect. Some Americans would be staying behind in Bonn because the German Defense Ministry was not moving to Berlin.

Before departing Bonn there were a few circumstances that were serious and cause for prayer. First, there was the downing of Korean Airlines Flight 007 over the Sea of Japan by Russian fighter aircraft on September 1, 1983. The flight was carrying 246 passengers and a crew of 23. Through a series of errors as well as faulty equipment, the flight passed into Russian restricted airspace. There was a meeting in Montreal for an emergency session of the ICAO, the International Civil Aviation Organization at the request of the Republic of Korea. The Russian response was negative with contempt for the truth. Their opinion of the civilized world was equaled only by their disdain for helpless people like the passengers aboard flight

007. They reserved for themselves the right to live by one set of rules, insisting everyone else live by another. They were supremely confident their crime and cover-up would soon be forgotten, and things would go back to business as usual. This action became far from closed and follow-on actions have brought about long overdue reappraisal in countries all over the globe.

Soon after this event, Monique and I were at a formal German function in dress uniform. Monique left our position at our table to speak to a friend two tables away and in French described how terribly bad the Russians were for downing a civilian passenger jet. This was overheard by the Russian Attaché seated nearby. He obviously understood French as well as German for he glared at me in response. You see, it was the German practice to use the same seating arrangements at various functions so one got accustomed to our respective surroundings and accommodations. In group meetings like formal affairs, I was the recipient of very cold stares (angry glares) that reflected the nature of Russian military personnel at that time. One might say that it exists yet today with the Russian unprovoked attacks on Crimea and Ukraine. Biblically, are we to understand the signs (*circumstances*)of the times in Ezekiel 38 and 39 where Russia along with others will be attacking Israel? My interaction with the Chinese Ambassador was much more amiable at that time. The social functions of our respective positions brought us into contact with many foreign dignitaries.

Second, there was the 1983 Beirut Marine barracks bombing. The terrorist attacks against U.S. and French armed forces in Beirut on October 23, 1983, claimed 299 lives. Because there were several State Department personnel from Bonn on temporary duty there, it was most appropriate to occasion a memorial with prayer at the embassy to pay homage to the fallen. The suicide bombing of the U.S. embassy represented a sea change in tactics for militia groups and terrorist organizations in the Middle East.

The occasion for serious prayer also occurred when Monique was diagnosed with stage four cancer in 1984 and was evacuated to Walter Reed in Washington D.C. for treatment. I accompanied her as an assistant. Fortunately, we had Monique's niece staying with us in Bonn to mind household affairs along with the supervision of our teen-age daughter Nathalie. I remember well the Easter Sunrise Service on the grounds of Walter Reed hospital. Besides celebrating our risen Christ, I was in prayer for Monique's healing.

I need to mention here that our son Thierry has been attending college at Florida State University. His fame during this period grew but not necessarily for the good for his mischievous side became somewhat unfavorably renowned.

My follow-on assignment was in the office of (ODECSOPS) Deputy Chief of Staff Operations, Pentagon. This brought about another change for our children. Nathalie's move was to Tallahassee where she was met by her brother and enrolled at FSU. Monique and I settled into a townhouse located in Burke, Virginia, a bedroom community to many who served at the Pentagon. The Duerr's, friends from Bonn, recommended the ideal location and included me in their carpool to the Pentagon.

One could characterize an assignment such as this as writing decision papers, preparing briefings, time in line at the copy machine, and long days of life at the Pentagon. Of a more serious note, I was located in a section that was conducting reviews of the various branches of the Army to determine equipment needs that matched developing tactical and strategic operations. At the time, I was handling Aviation which had recently become a branch, of Military Police, and Total Systems

Material Acquisitions, which was a catch-all to meet Department of Defense (DoD) Acquisitions. This Acquisition Process was one of three (3) processes (Acquisition, Requirements, and Funding) that made up and supported the Defense Acquisition System and was implemented by DoD Instruction 5000.02. These instructions along with 5000.85 Major Capability Acquisition provided the policies and principles that govern the defense acquisition system and form the management foundation for all DoD programs.

Material acquisition is much more complicated than that which I briefly described and then there was the cherry blossom scramble that we experienced. Congressional changes to the Defense budget reverberated down through the Pentagon, especially during the cherry blossom season which caused long days in fashioning changes to programs and priorities. There is a course of study that used to be a specialty (54). This course covers the details of how the Pentagon or rather how the Defense Department works. Too graph this process system from the beginning to completion is mind-boggling. This is the serious side of assignment to the Pentagon.

There was also a lighter side to this posting for it was amusing to hear snoring coming from one of the stalls in a restroom (Latrine). Not really the most comfortable location to catch some needed shut-eye. Shirley highway (I-95) South at various intersections was not conducive to rapid commutes at that time. The 12 miles home to Burke, Virginia often took an hour. This provided the time to snack and put-up window signs bearing our happenstance to be stuck in traffic.

It is time I explain why I chose to retire from the military at this time in 1985 verses going on to a thirty-year career. Foremost, in my mind was that by age because of my enlisted time I did not feel I would be competitive for further promotions. Second, to be available at a

Assignment at Pentagon and retirement from Army 1985

reasonable/marketable age for a follow-on civilian career, I believed it to be advantageous to retire after twenty commissioned years. In so doing, I had the opportunity to have two competing contracts for further employment outside the military. One was with FMC, a company that builds the Bradley Fighting vehicle located in San Jose, California. The other contract was with Singer Flight Simulation Division in Binghamton, New York.

After research, I chose Singer which had 65 K employees counting all their divisions at that time. Singer Flight Simulation may have been considered at that time, the jewel of the company. They also made the famous Singer sewing machine. In my mind more renowned than this was the Apollo 13 simulator, production F-16 simulators, prototype F-22 simulator as well as multiple contracts for UH-1 Huey flight simulators which I had logged countless hours flying under simulated instrument conditions. The B-52, B-1B as well as the AH-64 simulators were also in their history and production. My lofty title in New Business Development was Staff Scientist.

Spiritual life in Binghamton, N.Y. was sort of hap hazard. In fact, I was saddened when attending Centenary United Methodist Church. Here is this big, beautiful sanctuary able to seat a thousand and yet had a small attendance of less than one hundred. Hand-crafted oak woodwork adorned the balconies as well as the alter area housing this very large, beautiful pipe organ. Granted, there was insufficient parking for all who preferred to drive to church by the present-day highways and byways. I suspect in its day downtown; apartment dwellers walked the few blocks to church.

A significant cause for prayer during this period was the Challenger explosion on January 28, 1986. There was not any corporate call for prayer by management but several of us employees prayed. The space program was close to Singer's defense programs.

It was about 1987-88 that Paul Bilzaren, a wealthy Floridian did a leveraged buyout of Singer stock and placed the respective divisions up for sale. CAE, a Canadian firm purchase Singer Flight Simulation Division which then lost its defense contracts. This caused a significant downturn in business and a reduction in the number of employees. This occurred in 1990. I was fortunate to sell our home in a matter of three weeks.

I need to mention that while in Binghamton, N.Y. our daughter Nathalie joined us and completed her last two years at the State University of New York at Binghamton in nursing and received a direction commission as a lieutenant in the Air Force. This made her father very proud and happy.

I interviewed with several defense firms around the U.S. however, we decided to move back to Florida. Monique settled into employment with Archbold Hospital in Thomasville where she had prior employment. I eventually attained employment with the Florida State Department of Elder Affairs, a new department destined to consolidate all programs dealing with the elder Floridian.

Why Tallahassee Florida? Well, our children and I had gone to school there and I was not particularly interested in starting some other place new where we did not know anyone. Our son Thierry was taking me around looking for homes and we found one that he had looked at for himself before on Lake Iamonia, about 12 miles North of city limits at that time.

TIME WITH CHRIST JESUS

Arise, shine (be radiant with the glory and brilliance of the Lord); for your light has come, and the glory of the Lord rises above you.

Isaiah 60:1 NIV

Let me go back to "NO GREATER LOVE HATH MAN THAN THIS, THAT HE LAY DOWN HIS LIFE FOR A FRIEND. John 15:13. For a very long time my trust in God was that if I was willing to die, lay down my life for him I would be okay. It was later that God gave another better understanding of this passage. That is to deny oneself as the Apostle Paul did. When I thought about the difference, I came to realize that it would be far easier to die for a friend than to deny oneself. To die for a believer or Christ is an easy one-time event often in combat without pain. To deny oneself is a continuous lifestyle that is a constant reminder throughout the day and the days to come. This requires behavior modification to the nth degree accompanied by prayer. "And when he had called the people unto him with his disciples also, he said unto them, let him deny himself, and take up his cross, and follow me". Mark 8:34 NIV

"Trust in the Lord with all your heart and lean not on your own understanding: in all your ways submit to Him, and he will make your paths straight." Proverbs 3: 5-6 NIV

"I considered and observed on earth the following: The race doesn't go to the swift, nor the battle to the strong, nor food to the wise, nor wealth to the smart, nor recognition to the skilled. Instead, timing and *circumstances* meet them all". Ecclesiastic 9:11 NIV

This scripture in my mind more than any others on *circumstances* has considerably more depth of understanding of just how ultimately powerful our God is in directing the steps of mankind and world events to bring about the desired change our God wants. It was in the nineties that I enrolled in Discipleship One, a six-month church coarse mentored by our pastor Kelly Smith. This was followed by Discipleship Two lasting a year.

It was during this period our son Thierry went to the doctor and was diagnosed with a brain tumor. Our life of bliss and tranquility came to a sudden lurch in the goings and comings of events. Much of what occurred during this timeframe is found in the book about him, "Did You Know Thierry," available on Amazon.com. 17

It was also in the late 1990s that I began spending more time with the Lord. In fact, I thought it good to tithe time, which is 2 hours and 24 minutes a day. Along with time with Jesus, I began to fast one day a week. This lasted about three years and only stopped when someone at a church meeting, asked "why wasn't eating lunch?" I explained that it was my fast day. Well, the next question came, "how long have you been doing this?" I felt ashamed when I blurted out three years which I thought at the time was wrong in that it could be construed as boasting. 2 Cor 11 NIV

Time with Jesus increased after 2000 when I started going on Celebrate Jesus missions. This fit my calling which I was not initially aware of. In fact, I once asked a seasoned Assemblies of God (A/G) pastor in Sioux City, Iowa "Why aren't there more pastors with the gift of evangelism/witnessing Christ Jesus and the Cross?" He responded with, but there are. "One, they simply are not aware of the gift, or two, they are aware of the gift but afraid to use it." Well, that was me on both accounts. It was after I learned of my gift and during my Baptism of the Holy Spirit that my ears heard a voice, saying, "Understand, Feed My Sheep." John 21:15-17. The voice was firm and could not be misunderstood as a command.

Initially, I was afraid to use the gift. I asked myself, here I am a combat veteran, and I am afraid to witness Jesus who stood by me all these years. After praying all the way from Tallahassee to Leesburg, Florida in 2000 for my first CJ mission, we missionaries were counting off by threes to commence walking from house to house. I ended up with the host pastor and his wife. My prayer is, "thank you Lord they know how to do this." After about a block of homes, I volunteered to go to the door to explain the mission and offer prayer.

CELEBRATE JESUS MISSION EXPLANATION

History, The Celebrate Jesus ministry was founded in 1994 by Reverend Dr. Rob Frost, National Evangelist for the Methodist Church in England. It was brought to the United States in 1998 after a visit to London, England where 'Share Jesus' was established to counter the steady decline in church attendance. Based on Matthew 28:19 "Go, therefore, and teach all nations, baptizing them in the name of the Father, and of the

Son, and of the Holy Spirit." The Celebrate Jesus (CJ) Vision 'Statement is Equip People to Share the Gospel and Reach Neighbors.' The CJ mission is the hope of the world (As expressed at the 2006 Willow Creek Leadership Summit by Hill Hybels). Through the local church, the hands of Jesus actively reach out and his feet walk into the neighborhoods to reach the lost and hurting of this world.18

Implementation: Celebrate Jesus (CJ) mission is represented in and through prayer. It is an ongoing process birthed and led by the Holy Spirit. "Manifestation of the Holy Spirit is given to each one for the profit of all." 1 Corinthians 12:7

Conduct: Through a Celebrate Jesus mission the church can be intentional about reaching out into your neighborhood. As we went out into the community and met neighbors, God honored our obedience and assisted and strengthened us. (Philippians 4:13)

The key objectives of a CJ mission were to equip emerging evangelists by providing an Apostolic model of outreach ministry. CJ's mission models the belief that people must be connected both to Jesus and the local church. When it was operational, CJ mission would send a mission team to respective churches that had covenanted with CJ to walk alongside church members in a typical outreach effort. The mission team would assist, guide, and suggest ways to: Pray about your mission, host the church team, visit your neighborhood, prepare for a block party at the end of a mission week, and follow through with the neighbors the church met during a mission.

On occasion, I had been involved with single-church missions without the advantage of an outside mission team. This involved training the church mission team and applying the mission model on a reduced scale, which is reducing the number of sessions to an evening-only house-to-house contact with the neighborhood as opposed to a morning, afternoon, and evening session. This was accomplished at Killearn Lakes United Methodist Church as well as Gray Memorial Methodist Church in Tallahassee. There were other single-church missions, but they had the support of CJ Mission headquarters outside teams.

However, if the church was sufficiently large enough more sessions could be added by members taking off work during mission week. The CJ mission model can be adjusted to fit almost all circumstances. During the Tallahassee Mission in 2006, we had two small church teaming together to form a viable more powerful mission. It is normal to plan at least one year in advance to prepare, pray, and organize for a CJ mission. It is critically important for prayer warriors to pray for the presence of the Holy Spirit in homes, streets, parks, schools, police stations, fire stations public libraries, nursing homes, assisted living facilities, as well as other government build-ings. The church leadership team was comprised of persons with a desire to reach out to the community. This consisted of the (Host Pastor, Key Leader, and Coordinators for Prayer, Hospitality, Visitation, and Block Party, as well as a Follow-Through). Bi-weekly meetings began ideally one year in advance of set mission week. Weekly meetings were suggested two months or more in advance of mission week.

The promotion of the CJ mission was of equal importance. In Deland Florida, CJ Mission had a banner across downtown main street. Tallahassee mission was broadcast on Christian radio along with a full-page announcement and description in the local paper written by a reporter who accompanied a mission team visiting homes and businesses. Coral Springs, Florida church had distributed over 10,000 invitations. Inci-dentally, it was estimated that over 5,000 attended the block party as measured by the number of water bottles that were given out to attendees, two per person.

During the conduct of the mission, it was normal for the respective teams to meet back at church after each morning, afternoon, and evening session in the neighborhood to pray and testify to the experience by describing what had been referred to as "Glory Stories", in essence, miracles, *circumstances* where prayer was answered on the spot, the following day or week. Here is an example of one answered over time. It was reported from a church in Tallahassee during church services that and individual stood up and stated. "I am here today because someone from this church stopped by my home, gave me a prayer plant, and prayed for me. That was two years ago".

I believe it was in Jacksonville that we prayed for a woman who had obvious medical issues judging from the tubes running along her neck. In my notes that I found, I was guessing the couple to be in their thirties, much too young for perceived heart trouble. We prayed for her healing. The couple were church goers. Our team then proceeded down the street to a dead end and came back on the opposite side. Well, this woman named Leah came running out from her home and said, "I need to tell you that another team from your mission had stopped by her father's home in another area. The mission team there had prayed for their daughter's healing. Leah stated that she had been praying for her father's salvation for over twenty years and that day he had come to Christ.

It was on another mission where my grandson Christian was with me. As we started out stopping at the first home, we found out that we were on the wrong street. A woman answered the door. She said, "a mission team had stopped by her house yesterday." We turned to go away and find the correct street to begin. "Wait, the women said, yesterday another church team prayed that I would find employment, well I did, and I start this Friday."

How rapidly can prayer be answered? At the end of a cul-de-sac, a woman was outside her home with the hood of her auto raised. After introductions and describing our purpose, this woman asked? "Please pray for my car for it won't start". I was not used to praying for articles, but I did. It was about four or five homes down the other side of the cul-de-sac, and lunch time when I knocked on the door and a gentleman answered. After introductions and an explanation of our purpose, I commented on the number of autos in his driveway. He stated that he was a mechanic and brought some autos home to work on. I said to him "well, this lady down the street with her car hood up has a problem with her car starting". Before I spoke further, he was off walking toward that auto to address the issue. Coincidence, no, *circumstance* yes. When you put all the situations together you begin to understand how God works through prayer, time, and diligence.

Our team stopped at a home where four kids were playing out in the street. When we knocked at the door of a home near all these kids, a man answered with a phone in his hand. We described our CJ mission and church activities. The gentleman responded with, "See all those kids, I was on the phone when you knocked seeking a church that had vacation Bible school and you said your church has one starting next week and your church is just three blocks away." What a beautiful timely answer to prayer.

An elderly woman answered the knock on her door and was visibly upset when asked if we could pray for her. Her nine-year-old granddaughter had drowned recently. As we held hands our group prayed for comfort, understanding, and healing. She was interested in finding a church and plans on visiting Asbury church. Another elderly woman came to the door in a home with three grandchildren she was tending. She was very interested in vacation Bible School and plans on attending church herself where there is childcare.

I did take notice of the many homes where we visited that often children were being tended to by a grandparent. The good news here I suspect is that the children were being nurtured by one who may have been steeped in the love of Christ in their lives because that was the way it was in the fifties and sixties when the grandparent was growing up.

SHOCK OF 9/11

In reflecting back to the horror of the terrorist attacks of September 11, 2001, that left nearly 3,000 people dead in New York City, Washington, D.C., and Shanksville, I am still amazed at the travesty of the occasion. According to Pew Research, the enduring power of the September attack was clear: An over-whelming number of Americans were old enough do recall what they were doing when they heard the news. Yet today, an ever-growing number of Americans have no personal memory of that day.

A review of U.S. public opinion in the two decades since 9/11 reveals how a badly shaken nation came together, briefly, in a spirit of sadness and patriotism. The public initially rallied behind the wars in Afghanistan and Iraq, though support waned over time. This led to the chaotic departure of allied forces from Afghanistan. The rapid departure did not have to happen. A well-planned extended turn-over to an established regime, from hindsight, could have occurred. The U.S. may not have been winning a protracted conflict, but the area was to a large extent stabilized. Representative government was established and functioning at that time.

1 Pew Research September 2021 "Two Decades Later." 19

Where was I on that Tuesday, September 11, 2001? I was the Director of Human Resources in a Florida Department for which I can attribute the appointment to our son's influence within state government. On that occasion, or rather the following Friday I was requested to lead a memorial service for our headquarters at the flagpole at lunchtime. The request gave me about two hours to prepare. Keep in mind that I was not a seasoned minister at that time. I was simply a dedicated believer who practiced the love of Christ by leading Bible study at lunch time in a vacant room of the Florida Lottery. The word had apparently spread about this Bible study for a memorial request to come to me.

From memory now, I believe I, or rather God had given me a portion of Psalm 51 as a base for memorial words. Psalm 51: 10-17 Create in me a clean heart, O God; and renew a right spirit within me. Vs.11 Cast me not away from your presence, and take not your Holy Spirit from me. Vs 12 Restore unto me the joy of your salvation; and uphold me with your free spirit. Vs 13 Then will I teach transgressors your ways; and sinners shall be converted unto you. Vs 14 Deliver me from blood guiltiness, O God, you God of my salvation, and my tongue shall sing aloud of your righteousness. Vs 15 O Lord, open my lips, and my mouth shall sing aloud of your righteousness. Vs 16 For you desire not sacrifice, else would I give it: you delight not in burnt offering. Vs 17 The sacrifices of God are a broken spirit: a broken and a contrite heart, O God, you will not despise.

The words I spoke in addition to Psalms 51, I do not remember. I do remember closing in the Lord's Prayer which the Headquarters crowd of around 200 joined in. For that period, a Christian was led to believe that the event would cause a religious awakening in America. Maybe it did but if so, it only lasted a few weeks. A span of time far too short to be worthy of study by social scientists.

I reference this by Googling the subject on social media. The terrorist attacks of September 11, 2001, were without question the defining moment of the 21st century to date. In the wake of this national tragedy, many people exhibited renewed religious commitment.

According to Gallup polls, religious attendance the first weekend after the attacks was up six percent from the weekend before, Religious pundits proclaimed the last months of 2001 to be a time of unprecedented religious and spiritual revival in the United States. But not everyone bought into this appraisal of the situation. Indeed, by November polls were already indicating that church attendance had retreated to normal levels. Despite the immensity of the attacks and the considerable amount of public discourse regarding their religious and spiritual[1] implications for Americans, however, these simple church attendance figures are the basis for much of our social scientific knowledge about Americans' religious and spiritual responses to 9/11.

Throughout the history of the Bible, our God has used good and bad things to happen to nations to get their attention and bring them back into his fold as a shepherd gathers his sheep. Then, after a while, they wondered off again. It was sad that the return to the fold of spiritual wellness by the United States was so short-lived.

CELEBRATE JESUS MISSIONS

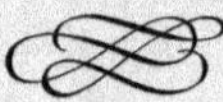

Now, I want you to know, brothers and sisters, that what has happened to me (*circumstances*) has really served to advance the gospel.

Philippians 1:13 NIV (Emphasis added)

Festival 2001 with Franklin Graham in Tallahassee was the next event in reflecting on how God uses *circumstances* to bring about His desired change to people, places, and nations whereby there is prayer.

In theology, Divine Providence, or simply Providence, is God's intervention in the Universe. The term Divine Providence is also used as a title of God.

So, can we not say God uses *circumstances* not only to bring about prayer but bring about His Divine Providence? I described a few of the events, *circumstance's* when I wrote in Janie Woodward's book, "Did you know Thierry"?

One event, *circumstance* was a meeting I attended with our son Thierry. It was an emergency meeting of about thirty pastors and church leaders to address the shortfall of the funds necessary for the Franklin Graham festival. This was about three weeks prior to the event. We were short $129,000. The discussion going around the room was about strategies that would address this issue. At the time Thierry, the Festival finance chair, proposed that each representative present write on a piece of paper a pledge that could be raised by their respective churches to cover the shortfall.

I wrote down what I believed our church could do. As the papers were collected one pastor present there mentioned that we should have written their church name down as well as the amount for accountability. The papers with pledge amounts were added up with a total amount coming to exactly $129,000. There was quiet reverence and prayer of thanksgiving for the odds of this occurrence were beyond human imagination. What God had done in that *circumstance* was show His divine power that I am sure resided well with all those present as witnesses.

After that meeting, Thierry had me drive him to a gated community address in Tallahassee of Tampa Bay's quarterback to pick up a large check. I was occasionally surprised and impressed by Thierry's influence.

Both Monique and I were at this time driving our son to appointments and meetings. His cancer diagnosed in 1999 was returning and he could no longer drive. The glioblastoma multiforme grade IV cancer had a reported 2% survival rate and he was succumbing to the physical debilitating effects of the disease.

The amazing thing during this illness was that Thierry did not experience an anxious moment throughout his illness. He attributed this *circumstance* to God's grace and love for him. In fact, at the time I thought he was handling all this medical drama better than Monique and me. It is natural for a parent to spiritually suffer for the illness of a child. The Word of God tells us this is the case over and over. Again, I reference the book, "Did You Know Thierry" by Janie Woodard.

Did not our hearts not weep and wax sore for Monique and me as well as for Diane, Thierry's wife? It had been nearly two years before when he was first operated on that we believed he would be healed. His going to be with the Lord on January 16, 2002, was then in our minds much too soon. Thierry, when able, would go from church to church, organization to organization like Rotary, Lions club, Kawana's, and more celebrating God's healing power. Now, in reflection on writing about the *circumstance*, I can better understand that it was in God's plan all along to use his exuberance, tenacity, and untimely death for the furtherance of His word.

One of the stories that did not make it into the book about him but was remembered by a brother was that which occurred with our daughter Nathalie. She was attending church in the vicinity of Tyndall Air Force Base near Panama City, Florida. At the conclusion of the Sunday school class, there was a call for prayer requests or testimonies.

A man in the class stated that he had a testimony that took place in Tallahassee, FL. He had lost his job and eventually lost his home. His wife and family had left him as well. He decided that he would have breakfast and then commit suicide. Well, at breakfast he met a man who was full of the love of Christ, exuberant and apparently of need to tell people how great our God is. He listened for a while and then gave his life to Christ. Since that encounter with this man, he had obtained a good job and his family had come back to him.

Our daughter asked that he describe this man who talked to him about Jesus' love and salvation. Well, he said that this man only had months to live because of a brain tumor but where he was going was a better place. Oh, and his name had a different spelling of Terry. Our daughter responded softly "that man was my brother."

My, how God puts things together that cause supernatural occurrences with purposeful meaning. All things work together for those who love the Lord and believe. Romans 8:28.

I wrote in Thierry's book about Randy's story because our son was involved with praying for Randy while he was well enough. I did not want to go into detail for it was not my wish to detract from our son's story. Now, I desire to add to the story about Randy. You see it was a period of time that from 1990 on that I was spending much more time with the Lord. In fact, I had begun tithing time to the Lord.

Randy was the Director of the CBS sports affiliate in Tallahassee. I worked with Johnna his wife at the Florida Lottery. When Johnna mentioned that her husband started feeling soreness in his shoulder, I told her I would stop by their home and pray for him. Over the course of two years his disease of Amyotrophic Lateral Sclerosis (ALS), commonly referred to as Lou Gehrig's disease became increasingly worse. Randy was raised as a Catholic but was not really that inclined or not a regular church goer.

When I started seeing Randy, his life, and direction could be explained as worldly, that is without spiritual direction. Often when I came by his home, it was un-godly programs that were on the TV set, and it was difficult to draw his attention to spiritual wellness. It was finally, after a year of visits with his condition worsening that he became more receptive to God's word. About this interval, I loaned a copy of the audio Bible on diskettes for him to listen to in my absence. His condition then was such that he was bed ridden and his voice had become extremely weak. A liquid diet was started by feeding through a tube to his stomach. His throat had to be suctioned periodically to remove phylum from his throat so he would not choke.

The small movement at that time was with much pain and suffering. Johnna arranged to have a gurney moved to the converted porch which facilitated Randy's care by a caregiver. Randy's communication now was only through blinking his eyes for yes or no, combined with an alphabet chart where words were spelled out for his response.

A most unusual feeding plan was worked out for the family. The Catholic church supplied a meal a week as well as my church and because of our son, the Baptist church was involved. Three different denominations were involved with his family caring. You see Johnna was still employed at the time, and the benevolence was needed to sustain the family.

I believe it was at least a year that Randy had been on this liquid meal plan. I was impressed with the number of stacked boxes in the garage to support this plan. One can only imagine the psychological as well as the physical strain that Randy and his family were going through during this period. Much had to do with a strong character and will to survive hour after hour of suffering and live. It is my belief from all of this was to realize what God has us endure until we come willingly unto Him. The Hymn, "Come Thou Fount of Every Blessing".

"Come Thou Fount of Every Blessing" is a Christian hymn written by the pastor and hymnodist Robert Robinson, who penned the words in the year 1758 at the age of 22.[1][2]

Come, Thou Fount of every blessing,

 Tune my heart to sing Thy grace;

Streams of mercy, never ceasing,

  Call for songs of loudest praise.

Teach me some melodious sonnets,

  Sung by flaming tongues above.

Praise the mount, I'm fixed upon it,

  Mount of Thy redeeming love.

Sorrowing I shall be in spirit,

  Till released from flesh and sin,

Yet from what I do inherit,

  Here Thy praises I'll begin;

Here I raise my Ebenezer;

  Here by Thy great help, I've come;

And I hope, by Thy good pleasure,

  Safely to arrive at home.

Jesus sought me when a stranger,

  Wandering from the fold of God;

He, to rescue me from danger,

  Interposed His precious blood;

How His kindness yet pursues me

  Mortal tongue can never tell,

Clothed in flesh, till death shall loose me

I cannot proclaim it well.

O to grace how great a debtor

Daily I'm constrained to be!

Let Thy goodness, like a fetter,

Bind my wandering heart to Thee.

Prone to wander, Lord, I feel it,

Prone to leave the God I love;

Here's my heart, O take and seal it,

Seal it for Thy courts above.

O that day when freed from sinning,

I shall see Thy lovely face;

Clothèd then in blood-washed linen

How I'll sing Thy sovereign grace;

Come, my Lord, no longer tarry,

Take my ransomed soul away;

Send thine angels now to carry

Me to realms of endless day.

The original text[3] of the hymn "Come Thou Fount of Every Blessing"

On one occasion I commented to Randy that he had the appearance of Christ. His open robe gave evidence of his struggle to simply breath. His bearded face displayed pain and agony. There was a cool wet towel across his forehead for his headache. His hair had grown long and was damp with sweat. I do not know if it was this time or another where through his charting alphabet, he described a dream he had of Christ washing his feet on the banks of the Euphrates River. For me, it was a good sign that Randy had accepted Christ as his Lord and Savior and was destined for heaven.

I do not remember how long it was after this episode that I was with Randy, and he motioned for his boys and the caregiver to leave the room. Then, I was in prayer, kneeling at the foot of his gurney. I had taken his bare feet in my hands as I had done recently. I had also been studying healing prayer over the past few months at that time. I do remember that it was necessary to go to Christ Jesus as pure at heart and mind as possible and I began praying. As I progressed, I asked Christ Jesus to forgive me for having a grudge against one of my brothers. It was not anger or hate, but simply a grudge. The grudge was over a simple plaque that was promised to me that he had taken from our home when our father had passed away. Wow, I hadn't even thought that was important and why under these *circumstances* was it to get voiced by my lips? Forgiveness in this instance, no matter how big or small is extremely important to God Almighty.

All of a sudden, from the periphery of my closed eyes, waves of rushing water came upon me followed by a surge of power entering my head. This power went through my torso down my arms into my hands holding Randy's feet. In a surprised now open eyes, I asked Randy if he had felt what just occurred. With wide open eyes, he blinked YES.

Accompanying this baptism of the Holy Spirit were the words my ears heard. "Understand, Feed My Sheep". By this time, I am weeping and thanking God for His healing power. I left Randy that day truly believing he would be physically healed. I have since come to understand he was Spiritually healed. You see it was not but three weeks later, on a Sunday morning that Johnna, his wife called to tell me that Randy had passed away.

The other remembered phenomime of the baptism of the Holy Spirit was the understanding that my sin body needed washing/cleansing before the Holy Spirit could enter it. Were these not the waves of water by vision that were at that time washing over me? There were more wows to follow at Randy's funeral in which I was to participate. Before the event, one of Randy's sons came and told me that he had something important for me to know. He was getting ready for the funeral and asked his brother what time it was for his watch had stop. His brother replied that it appeared his watch had stopped so they asked the care giver what time it was. Both the boy's watches were once their father's. The caregiver's watch had stopped as well at five. All three-time pieces had Roman numbers on their watch face. The boys agreed that it was their dad who kept asking them to put Roman's five on the diskette player for him to hear over and over. I used this information in my funeral eulogy as well as at the Lottery when Johnna was being honored at her departure. I later found in my log the occasion (*circumstance*) that I had read Romans V to Randy on a visit.

FRANKLIN GRAHAM FESTIVAL

Now, so that you also may know about my *circumstances* as to what I am doing, Tychicus, the beloved brother and faithful servant in the Lord, will make everything known to you.

Eph 6:21

It seems appropriate here to relate to a portion of my devotional, "The Utmost for His Highest" by Oswald Chambers. The Beatitudes found in Matthew 5:3-10 contain the dynamite of the Holy Ghost. They explode, as it were when the *circumstances* of our lives cause them to do so. When the Holy Spirit brings to our remembrance of these Beatitudes we say- "What a startling statement that is!" and we must decide whether we will accept the tremendous spiritual upheaval that will be produced in our *circumstances* if we obey His words. That is the way the Spirit of God works. We do not need to be born again to apply the Sermon on the Mount literally. The literal interpretation of the Sermon on the Mount is child's play; the interpretation by the Spirit of God as He applies our Lord's statements to our *circumstances* is the stern work of a saint.

The teaching of Jesus is out of all proportion to our natural way of looking at things and it comes with astonishing discomfort to begin with. We have slowly formed our walk and conversation on the line of the precepts of Jesus Christ as the Holy Spirit applies them to our *circumstances*. The Sermon on the Mount is not a set of rules and regulations: it is a statement of the life we will live when the Holy Spirit is getting His way with us.

The Franklin Graham Festival 2001 in Tallahassee was mentioned in our son's book particularly the number of miracles that occurred leading up to and during this event for the precision.

This particular song comes to mind to describe how God through circumstances finds a way to bring about change.

Song by Don Moen

Lyrics

God will make a way
Where there seems to be no way
He works in ways we cannot see
He will make a way for me
He will be my guide
Hold me closely to His side.
With love and strength for each new day
He will make a way, He will make a way.
(Sing it together)
Oh, God will make a way
Where there seems to be no way
He works in ways we cannot see
He will make a way for me
He will be my guide
Hold me closely to His side.
With love and strength for each new day

He will make a way, He will make a way
By a roadway in the wilderness, He'll lead me
(Rivers in the desert)
Rivers in the desert will I see
Heaven and earth will fade but His Word will still remain.
And He will do something new today
Oh, God will make a way
Where there seems to be no way
He works in ways we cannot see
He will make a way for me
He will be my guide
Hold me closely to His side.
With love and strength for each new day
He will make a way, He will make a way
Who might be here tonight
You may think God has forgotten you
About your situation, but He hasn't
The Bible says that we are inscribe in the palm of His hand
And Heaven and earth may pass away
But His word will remain forever
And He can do exceedingly, abundantly
Above all that we could ever ask or think tonight (amen)
Amen, let's sing it
Oh, God will make a way
Where there seems to be no way
He works in ways we cannot see
He will make a way for me
He will be my guide
Hold me closely to His side
With love and strength for each new day
He will make a way, He will make a way
With love and strength for each new day
He will make a way, He will make a way

It was a long week-end of spiritual festivities that included a chorus of hundreds of singers from many churches who had practiced a number of times leading up to the event. There was a children's program with "Bible Man" including a call for children to give their lives to Christ.

The whole event was five years in the development and implementation involving the whole Tallahassee community. The festival 2001 by the numbers was quoted from Tallahassee Democrat provided by Sherman Barnette, festival director.

1,000 people in the choir.

231 participating Big Bend, Florida churches

300 ushers

600 spiritual counselors greeted and directed each person who went to the stage to make a commitment to Jesus.

200 co-laborers, behind-the-scenes clerical workers.

15,00 seats in the exhibit hall. The festival outcome could not be measured by human minds, but better by the rejoicing in heaven by a host of angles for the number of people that had given their lives to Christ. 20

Monique and I had two grandchildren, Christian and Nicole give their lives to Christ during the session with 'Bible Man'. This was cherished by us for the time and the times to come.

LIFE AS A MISSIONARY

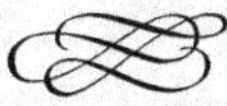

For I have sent him to you for this very purpose, that you may know about our *circumstances* and that he may encourage your hearts.

Col 4:8

The scripture is part of the apostle Paul's final greeting in the midst of some turmoil where he sought to explain that Christ is the Creator and sustainer of the universe, the redeemer of sinners, and the head of the Church. Yet there is a glorious, previously unrelated mystery in the reality that Christ dwells in every believer as the Hope of glory. That believers will appear with the risen Christ in glory; Col 3:4 is a powerful incentive for godly living.

I wish to return to Celebrate Jesus missions which continued in Florida followed by a few in Georgia. This activity is described in a letter I wrote to the district shortly after the district meeting where I had a Celebrate Jesus Missions booth. Each missionary during one of the concluding sessions was given a short time to describe his/her mission before the audience of church attendees.

Copy of Letter.

Gene Kobes
10670 Lake Iamonia Drive
Tallahassee, FL32312
Pastor Tommy Moore Superintendant, West Florida District
Council of the Assemblies of God
4792 Highway 90 Marianna, FL 32446
RE: Things I Did Not Say in 30 Seconds

Dear Brother Moore,

I humbly very much appreciated the opportunity to participate in the West Florida District Council meeting in Mariana and address the gathered banquet, however, I will confess that I was struggling to find just the right short 30-second time allotted spot to describe the Celebrate Jesus Mission (CJ Mission) since we are the new kid on the block. Other ministries present there have a rich history, staffed by generations of Pentecostals and it was interesting to hear an update of their accomplishments.

So, what element of the CJ mission would most appropriately describe or relate to the mission of the district? What could I say that would review the short time attendees spent at the CJ mission booth so it would rest on their hearts? Celebrate Jesus does not have a storied history of accomplishments. Even though God fits all things together for his purpose, we live in a world where we still manage to measure and compare what we think is important in or to our ministry.

So, I am telling this story of what is on my heart that I did not have time over the past three days to tell. You see, rather than in normal early morning Bible study I was fretting off and on about what I did not say until God let me know that I should simply write it down and send it off to the district.

I did not talk about the point that you need to go on a CJ mission before you think you could host a mission at your church. This makes sense. It is critically important to learn about the details of an effective mission before you attempt to expend the energy and resources on something that just maybe fails to meet your expectations. Ah, but I am glad that I did not talk about this at the banquet for that sounds like a wet blanket in 30 seconds or less.

I did not give an example of how in Okeechobee we drove church kids out to the farms of unchurched friends/classmates where we gave these friends a small gift, invited them to the block party, and prayed with them. No, we did not cover a lot of homes that day but it was effective. I suspect this would be an effective method of reaching those in the sparsely populated areas of our district. It was heartwarming to see and participate in a group of teenagers along with parents joining hands in prayer.

I did not have time to talk about the time while handing out cold bottled was at a pharmacy that we observed a man in a closed auto across the street. Now, it is July in South Flor-ida, and this did not look right. The two missionaries walked over and tapped on the window. There was little movement, so the door was opened and an EMT was called. After the gentleman was picked up by an ambulance, we checked the hospital the following day and found out that he had suffered a heart attack for which he was being treated.

I did not relate to the time in North Port when we were in the police station praying with officers on duty. By the way, it is our practice to join hands while in prayer. We had just dropped off some cookies. Anyway, I noticed a young girl of maybe fifteen or sixteen sitting by herself along the wall. The plain-clothed officer beside her was probably waiting for us to leave before booking her for some offense. I walked over to her, knelt down and asked her if I might pray for her. She gave me her hand and I began to pray. Now, I was doing alright until she began to cry so uncontrollably. Then, I began to weep in prayer. In these circumstances, you lose track of time in prayer. "God almighty help this child in trouble. Forgiver her sins and guide her unto the paths of righteousness for your namesake and more." There was more but this much I remembered.

I did not have the time to talk about the time in Miami when my grandson and I started off that morning session on the wrong street. It was really Coral Springs, which is by itself a large city. Anyway, at the very first home we came to a woman answered the door. Before I could finish our introduction, she stated, "Someone with a shirt like yours was here yesterday." I replied that I was sorry and started to leave but she stopped me with, "wait, don't go away, let me tell you the three people prayed for me. They prayed that I would find a job. Well, that afternoon I was called and informed that I would be hired and I start work tomorrow". We called these answered prayers, "Glory Stories". During mission, God gives us feedback during our encounters that he is at work answering prayer requests. Sometimes it is immediate, sometimes the next day, during the week, or even later that we find out. I like the circumstances that occurred in Tallahassee during a single church mission there. I was told by a member of my old church that there was a person in church who gave a testimony. He said that he was there because two years ago someone from that church had stopped by his home, given him a prayer plant, and prayed with him. That was our mission. So, you do not measure a mission for its outcome the following week or two. God works in His own time but lovingly gives you feedback that prayers are answered.

I did not have the time to tell the story of the lady in Jacksonville who wanted our team to pray over her auto that would not start. She had to get to work. Well, it was not but a half block away that I commented to the induvial who was home that he sure had a collection of cars in his driveway. He explained that he was a mechanic, and he took some autos home to work on. Well, sir, I said there is this lady down the street that has this auto with the hood up for it won't start. Almost before I finished explaining, he was footing it down the street. This might seem somewhat light but it is so wonderful when steeped in answered prayer you do not know if the fatigue in you is physical or spiritual.

I did not encapsulate the week of 14-hour days the church prayer team prayed over the hundreds of prayer request cards. I did not mention the number of people who came to Christ during the mission week or during the follow-up. Oh, then there was the church in Deland that continued mission activities for three years after the event which was written up in their national denominational magazine. Perhaps that was influenced by the fact that all the churches along with the hospital in Deland participated in the CJ mission that year led by First Assembly of God in Deland. What about the mission in Jacksonville where in a session of the 29 homes where there was someone at home during our visit 28 prayers were requested at the door? There is much brokenness out there and with each session (three a day) there is utter exhaustion after a week. Why did I not capture the continuous prayer and weeping that goes on during a CJ mission week in 30 seconds at our W. Florida District meeting?

As a Team Leader one past summer, I made my second pre-mission trip to Smyrna, Georgia the last weekend in April. There I was shown the neighborhoods that were planned for the mission. The Key Leader took me through a mobile home park that she said she had already prayed over several times. You see, the host church prays over the area prior to the mission. Their prayer warriors, and prayer walkers pray the Holy Spirit is presents in the area preparing the hearts, minds, and souls of the families before the missionaries go through the neighborhoods. One particular mobile home had a sign taped to the front of the home, BLIND PERSON. There was a string from the door to the mailbox to guide the individual. Need I say more?

Let me interject here that before our district commencement in Mariana, Pastor Larry gave me five minutes of pulpit time to encourage CJ's mission sigh-up. Bulletin stuffers, mission applications as well as a new display booth were all part of the service. Well, our assembly has gotten pretty used to my plea for participation in the summer missions. Freedom church has sent as many as eleven on missions besides hosting a mission in 2006 in which eight other churches in the area participated.

How can our assembly be energized one more time? Pastor Larry at an earlier service talked about a retold story that an individual had heard before. He said you are not interested in hearing it again, unless-unless you are in the story. I thought about the song, "I love to Tell the Story". We believers are in the story but are we telling the story of Jesus and his love? Then with the microphone in hand, I appealed to the assembly to think back to when they were children and sang, "This Little

Light of Mine" I'm going let it shine, let it shine. We need to think again as children, unencumbered with the cares of this world, and let our light shine for the lost. Then as we do in CJ mission numbers with childlike expectation, we experience God as He is answering all these prayers lifted to him. Then we can sing, "I Got the Joy, Joy, Joy Down in My Heart, where, down in my heart, where? ---All around the neighborhood.

There are many, many, many other glory stories as well as many prayer requests that I did not have the time to tell. I did not even end my 30-second allowed time with, "I pray that you may be active in sharing your faith, so you will have a full understanding of every good thing we have in Christ Jesus". Philemon 1:6. The only thing the Holy Spirit placed on my lips in conclusion that evening of the banquet was the example of the old retired pastor who stated after my presentation at the door: "You know son, what you are doing is what we used to do back in the old days".

In Christ,

Gene Kobes
Outreach Ministries
CJ Mission Team Leader

After sixteen years of experience in CJ missions I have come to understand that you can preach evangelism, and teach evangelism in Sunday school, but it really doesn't happen until you experience evangelism. Military people should understand this along with other vocations. The Job Training (OJT) is a very good teacher if not the best teacher.

This thought is backed up by a quote from <u>The Assemblies of God: A Popular History</u> by Edith Baumhofer. "You cannot teach people to be a witness; they become witnesses when they have an experience of something... A good Pentecostal witness is one who can tell how he got saved, healed, and baptized in the Holy Spirit." When I preached on missions, it was to encourage the congregation to the extent possible to join us in visiting missionaries in house-to-house visits. By the way, when you experience evangelism, you are more than likely to increase your mission giving. Oh, and along the way my wife acquiesced to my call and accompanied me numerous times while prayer walking as did our daughter Nathalie.

In 2004 Dr. Eric R. Hallett examined Celebrate Jesus Mission with "An Exploration of Pastoral Experiences" in his dissertation presented to the Faculty of Asbury Theological Seminary. In summary, I am providing some of the findings. 21

1. Pastors described that they were stretched in their understanding of the need to connect with people in the community.
2. CJ's mission seemed to offer a process for outreach that was action-oriented and team-oriented.
3. Many pastors expressed excitement and euphoria during the mission.
4. There were measurable results. From my experience, I witnessed increased attendance. Two churches in the Tallahassee area increased to the point of requiring new construction or a new larger campus.
5. Some lay participants of the CJ mission were encouraged to go into the ministry.
6. Many pastors experienced the Spirit of God moving in demonstratable ways which was surprising and new to them.
7. Most pastors reported God moving personally in their own lives.

8. The revelation to many of these pastors was that real people, in real churches, could see God at work.
9. Pastors reported with joy the ministry tasks that their faith through the execution of servant evangelism projects.
10. Pastors reported that the mission represented Christianity as presented by writers of the New Testament.
11. CJ pushed lay people to do things they had never done before.
12. Celebrate Jesus offered the participation component of outreach missions to be opened up to laypeople.
13. One of the core components of a Celebrate Jesus mission is the aspect of teamwork in the mission affirmed by pastors.
14. Finally, the theological implication was the discovery that CJ missions offered pastors and laypeople the freedom to invite anyone to their church even before they believed.

In the old method of evangelism in the Christendom model, you would hand someone a tract, and they would accept or reject it. This was "believe before you belong" evangelism. With Celebrate Jesus we invite people to belong before they believe. We want people to have a chance to "overhear" the gospel and see it lived out in the community and then have an opportunity to make a decision to accept Christ.

SERVING CHRIST JESUS

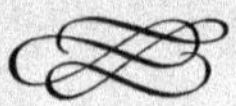

Abide in Me and I will remain in you. No branch can bear fruit by itself; it must remain in the vine. Neither can you bear fruit unless you remain in me.

John 15:5 NIV

We are not meant to be illuminated versions but the common stuff of ordinary life exhibiting the marvel of the grace of God. Drudgery is the touchstone of character. The great hindrance in spiritual life is that we look for big things to do. "Jesus took a towel and began to wash the disciples' feet." We need to remember to let God have His way with our lives. He is the one who is engineering our *circumstances.* I espouse these things because CJ's mission in Florida as an institution ended in 2016.

Questions may come about, if the Celebrate Jesus Missions were so great, why did they end? I believe they ended like many previous revivals. The people and the churches involved grew weary. CJ missions lasted eighteen years. Some writers indicate that it is God's will for them to end, and like seasons coming in and going out. Other writers have described revivals like waves, one wave comes in, and then it goes back out. If an individual or congregation isn't living in a revival state, are they not then lukewarm, complacent, apathetic, lethargic – asleep? No one would agree that it is God's will for His people.

We understand that we were not designed for constant mountain top experiences. The Christian life is much like those large, majestic mountains and lonely valleys. For you see, for every mountain there must be a valley. And, for every mountain-top Christian experience, we will certainly experience the valley as well. My experience as CJ missions were winding down was that the involved people simply grew tired, spiritually or physically. During the 18 years of missions, those with the will to continue had to pray unceasingly for the energy, vigor, enthusiasm, and love to experience the joy that comes from leading someone to Christ Jesus and the cross. I admit that I was physically drained after each mission. That is because the mission tempo (military term) for rate and endurance was exceedingly high. The participating churches were a flurry of activity leading up to, during, and after action or follow-up. When you are going house to house morning, afternoon, and evening praying, you are simply exhausted.

During the 2006 Tallahassee mission involving a total of nine churches where I was the area mission's leader, I lost my voice and could barely audibly pray during the block party while serving in the prayer tent. The designated prayer tent or room was my choice for mission block party assignments. That is where I could spiritually measure the impact of how God was working in the hearts and minds of those savoring the goodness of love, giving and pure comfort of God's glorious presence.

I believe it was in Coral Springs where the church I was assigned had a beautiful chapel set up for prayer. I stepped outside at one point to take a break and observed a young lady jumping up and down outside the window attempting to see what was going on. I invited her in and very quickly learned she could not speak English. I went outside where we had a loudspeaker, and the call went out for the Spanish-speaking pastor that was on our team. He arrived shortly and began talking in her native language. How much time passed, I do not know but the vision of this young lady kneeling at the alter and giving her life to Christ was one of serene beauty.

It was in Belle Glade where the church mission planning group had arranged bags of candy and goodies for each child that came to the prayer tent. My, I had a long line of children. After one child had left me, I asked him if he really knew Jesus. He turned as he was walking away and said, "Sure, He walks on water". Of all the affirmations I could have imagined that was one of the more definitive statements of understanding, trust, and obedience. I need to explain that during mission week, it was not uncommon to have been active in prayer and devotion for about seventeen hours a day. I checked my log for confirmation.

Yet before I close on CJ missions, there is one more occasion to account for which was at a Nazarene church in Jacksonville, Florida. Pre- mission meetings did not disclose the nature of the mission that was much different than any other or rather not even in the programed study or experience. Instead of going house to house as we normally did, the church host pastor enlisted us as visiting missionaries, our vehicles, along with a small bus to pick up 60 to 70 children in a depressed area. We transported them to church for a day of worship and children's Bible stories mixed with outdoor games. The area was predom-inately an ethnic minority. Children ranged from six or seven to teenage mothers who were nursing babies. My team of missionaries were middle-aged to elderly and not trained in children's church. Lunch was items provided by a government agency.

The church at that time did not have potable water, so we used only bottled water for hydration and brushing our teeth. Even so, one or two of my missionaries became ill. Outside afternoon games in 90-to-95-degree temperatures were extremely trying. The conditions wore on my team which needed my intervention on a number of occasions. There were no church staff available for support. The church only had staff for food preparation, so activities were handled strictly by myself along with seven missionaries. I was concerned that the whole operation could have been declared unsafe by authorities if investigated. I was transporting eight or nine kids in my five passengers auto.

It was Wednesday or Thursday noon that I went to my room to pray. As soon as my head hit my pillow, my mind was taken from me, and I could not think of a word of prayer. My mind simply stopped functioning. This was a scary situation that lasted I do not know how many seconds. I began to weep in utter humbleness as my mind came back and I uttered. "Lord, lord even in the heat of battle I could pray, what is happening?" I have since come to understand in reflection, whatever the *circumstances*, whatever spiritual mission you may be on if it is in God's name, He will overcome. Reference Romans 8:15, "And by him, we cry out Abba, Father." The Spirit himself testifies with our spirit that we are God's children." Romans 8:16

The *circumstance* above was obviously not subtle in any manner, but very dynamic so that it would be remembered throughout my life here on earth. I remain so very humbled by my God that it was deemed important for Him to capture my attention in the most powerful obedient manner.

There were other ministries that I guess by my nature and calling that I became involved with like Emmaus or another name Tres Deus (Three Days). My walk was the Big Bend (Florida) Walk to Emmaus number 16, Table of Matthew. The *circumstance* and true blessings were that the whole three days were bathed in prayer. Talks, discussion, meditation along sharing provided an atmosphere of sublime comfort and understanding of God and His love of humankind. Currently, I do not remember the number of Walks I have participated in both in Florida and Texas. From its humble beginning in Texas to a world-wide believer's institution, Emmaus is a sign of the work of the Holy Spirit in these last days. For those who have not heard or experienced the blessing of participation, it is gloriously refreshing. There are those who have come to accept Christ as their Lord and Savior through this ministry. I suspect this may be more the case for Kairos, the Walk tailored for prisons. There is also Chrysalis, a Walk for children.

The impact of this ministry is long-lasting. I have joined and remain in attendance with a cell group here in San Antonio that has been meeting for over twenty years from the time they went through Emmaus. Without giving too much away I would like to reference a song that I believe came to me through Emmaus:

Have you Seen Jesus, My Lord
Have you seen Jesus, my Lord? He's here in plain view.
Take a look, open your eyes. He'll show it to you.
Have you ever looked at the sunset, With the sky mellow
and red,
And the clouds suspended like feathers? Then I say you've seen
Jesus my Lord.
Have you ever stood at the ocean, With the white foam at your
feet, Felt the endless thundering motion? Then I say you've seen
Jesus, my Lord.

Have you ever looked at the cross, with a man hanging in pain?
And the look of love in His eyes? Then I say you've seen Jesus,
my Lord.
Have you ever stood in the family,
With the Lord there in your midst
Seen the face of Christ on your brother?
Then I say you've seen Jesus, my Lord.
Have you ever prayed for your church, With the Lord there in
your midst,
Seen the face of Christ on your sister? Then I say you've seen
Jesus, my Lord.

Oh, and then there were Christians United for Israel (CUFI) led by Pastor Hagee who launched this foremost Christion organization over fifteen years ago. Their mission is to educate and empower millions of Americans to speak and act with one voice in defense of Israel and the Jewish people. CUFI is committed to confronting indifferences and combating antisemitism in all its forms wherever it may be found.

My introduction and participation began when there was a Night to Honor Israel (NTHI) event in Tallahassee, Florida. This *circumstance* was a true blessing that was followed up by attending my first convention in Washington D.C. A few years later, my wife and I along with our twelve-year-old granddaughter Micah, attended another CUFI convention in D.C. I can date this convention because of Micah's age at the time 2014. At that time, I recall that the number of adherents was around six million nationwide. In 2024, the number has grown to over eleven million.

The *circumstance* that I fondly refer to was refreshed recently. It was a Night to Honor Israel on the Florida State University campus. Mr. Eric Stackelbeck, Trinity Broadcasting Network (TBN), from "The Watchman Program", was the keynote speaker. There were approximately twenty Palestinian demonstrators in attendance. Following the ceremony and talks, the Palestinians began chanting slogans of protest on the street below the union meeting hall. Soon thereafter a group of Israeli students on a balcony above the demonstrators began singing a Hebrew hymn. I did not understand Hebrew but believed it to be a song of deliverance.

You can read hymns of praise and deliverance in the old and new Testaments but to see and experience the *circumstance* is a demonstration of beauty and humble adoration. Then, as recently as last week while viewing an update of the current conflict in Israel on YouTube, the video captured a squad of Israeli soldiers singing a hymn of what I suspect was one of deliverance before going into battle.

Have you ever experienced a time in your life when you were going through a difficulty, and the Holy Spirit brought to your attention a song or hymn that has brought you through trouble in those times of distress and difficulty? I have, and a song comes to mind that comforts and fits the *circumstance*. Praise is also a weapon and there is power in praise. Praise the Lord oh my soul, and all that is within me praise His Holy Name. Psalm 103:1. The Lord surrounds us with songs of deliverance. Psalm 37:7

Then in the New Testament, Paul and Silas are praying and singing hymns while in a Philippian prison. After an earthquake and binding chains were broken as well as cell doors opened, the jailer asked Paul what he must do to be saved. Acts 16:23-40.

Why now, except by *circumstances* do I remember as of recent, 'The Battle Hymn of the Republic'. Perhaps because wherever I searched on YouTube there were many programs of worship music from around the world. From the West Point academy orchestra and singers to the Garden Tomb, the song of Moses in Hebrew. Hallelujah, and My Prayer by world-class vocalist as well as an orchestra of one hundred harps filled the evening for Monique and me. Oh, then there was the Jesus Christ Superstar concert that just came back from memory. God must surely love the music of praise and adoration glorifying His Holy Name.

SPIRITUAL DREAMS

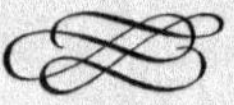

Now I want you to know, brothers and sisters, that my *circumstances* have turned out for the greater progress of the gospel.

Philippians 1:12

It was early spring in 2011 that Monique and journeyed to France to celebrate our fifty years of marriage. We were walking about memory city, Poitiers, rekindling places we visited like the Kaserne where I was stationed. Monique's stepbrother, a retired LT Colonel in the French army got us access because it was still being used as a base for their troops. A new mess hall and club, (dinning facility) were constructed right next to the old finance office where I worked. We had lunch there which far outshone any military meals I remembered. The old service club where I had a part-time job was converted into a gymnasium. When the manager asked what our purpose was in our visit, I described in French that Monique and I were celebrating our anniversary and I was once stationed there fifty years ago. He gave me a microphone and stated, "tell all present exercising here the *circumstances*."

He then proceeded to show me around the facility. Through the back door was an old horse barn still in condition to be used. In the two years I was stationed there I never knew that structure existed. The theatre was closed along with the snack bar. The old mess hall was converted to storage as well as the Post Exchange (PX). Besides the new dinning facility, all other structures were still in use as I remembered them. It was like a lost-in-time vision of things that were and still are.

The Chapel where Monique and I were married was locked during our visit, but a new glass door indicated it was still in use. Before leaving the area, I walked out the gate to the head of the 214 worn stone stairs we descended to walk about the city. Later, our young bodies had to climb this stairway and make it back to the castle after an evening on the town. If it was after midnight without a pass, there was this point along the walled casern where we could climb over the wall by way of a concrete poll. Incidentally, the stairway was the shortcut for the winding road that meandered down the hilltop.

I do not remember if it was this European vacation or an earlier one, however, it was a time when the cherry trees in my mother-in-law's garden were just ripe for picking. So, I believe it was one of Monique's nephews and I were up in the tree picking cherries and I was eating some as I climbed from limb to limb. It was later that evening; I was coming down with the flu by way of a fever. After a couple of days, we were at the doctor's office to find out it wasn't the flu but something perhaps a little more serious. So, I was taken to a French hospital in Cahors, France by ambulance.

The pain I was experiencing was significant and I was in prayer. As the day grew long and through the night, I prayed for deliverance and healing. I do not to this day know that my prayers were ever so fervent and unceasingly over the course of days before my pain ceased. It was determined that I had been poisoned by the insecticide that was used in a vineyard next to my mother-in-law's garden. The wind must have carried the insecticide to her garden cherry trees.

Now, about a month later, I was back in the United States, and I was on a mission in South Florida. After a few hours of outside labor in a shut-in's yard, I had a relapse of my illness. Again, I was in pain and prayed that Friday afternoon during the block party as well as through the night. The next day I was too sick to eat any meal. Prayer was again fervent as the illness did not subside until late the following day. Eventually, I was healed without any lingering illness or disability. "Thank the Lord, oh my soul and all that is within me bless His Holy Name, for He is a loving God and Healer."

Monique has reminded me that it was perhaps not that vacation to France but an earlier one, however, the memory of that *circumstance* remains with me. During this period of time, I had been serving on Emmaus Walks which are staffed by volunteers on various committees. When not in a leadership role, I would volunteer for the prayer committee for which I felt conditioned. This committee prays over the duration of the walk (three days). It is very exhausting, but likened to CJ missions which last seven days.

Just as CJ missions were concluding in Orlando and Tallahassee I was selected as the Para church coordinator for the Franklin Graham Fifty state Decision America Tour for Florida. Oh, by the way, I had been studying for a number of years to become a credentialed minister and was after a time approved as a U.S. Missionary in the Assemblies of God for church Plants and Development. Eventually, I concluded my credentialing by completing my coursework in 2018 and ordained in 2019. It was reported by the Assemblies of God at least for that year that I was the oldest ordained candidate to be credentialed. It was not my intention to set records, but it was a unique miracle that occurred during the written portion of my finale exam. You see, there was this room of perhaps thirty-plus students taking exams at various levels of certification. I was on the last question of the exam where we were to write a synopsis of our respective calling. It was during a rainstorm in that area of San Antonio and unbeknownst to the church, there was a significant leak in the roof and the ceiling tile directly above my desk gave way releasing about a glass of water ruining the ability to write any more in my exam booklet. The classroom attendant allowed me to submit a typed copy of my calling to complete the examination. It was later that I came to understand that my ordination was anointed. How else can you explain this *circumstance* without boasting? I was immensely humbled by the occurrence.

Another circumstance likened to the one above is that which occurred at the kitchen table where early morning, I read my Bible and prayed. My Bible at that time was a Fire Bible edition with a Bible jacket that had pockets. As I opened my Bible that morning, an unzipped pocket allowed my anointing oil purchased in Israel to fall out and drop to the tile floor at my feet. The broken vial released a beautiful fragrant aroma that seemed to last until my scriptural reading was complete. Again, I was dynamically humbled. One might say, well that was just a simple accident. I respond with. "No, especially when the Holy Spirit is involved anointing your feet with olive oil."

Here it seems appropriate to write down a few of my dreams. One night while deep in sleep my ears heard a voice that said, "Read Zephaniah". "I asked or stated in my dream, "Why Zephaniah, a minor prophet?" "The voice again repeated more firmly, read Zephaniah, then read the seventh book of the Bible." In my dream, I am counting off the books of the Bible. Genesis, Exodus, Leviticus, Numbers, Deuteronomy, Joshua and then I could not think of Judges but told the voice I would comply and read Zephaniah and the seventh book when I was awake.

Zephaniah, according to Tim LaHaye's study Bible is 89% prophecy which places the book just behind Revelations which is 95% prophecy. Like Isaiah fifty years before him, the inspired prophet looks beyond the immediate situation to focus frequently on the future, "Day of the Lord," those events in Judah that would soon foreshadow another key element of Zephaniah's teaching. That is the concept of a remnant who is protected in the day of the Lord. (Zeph. 2:7; 3:13). The day of the Lord's prophecies in 1:14-18 will be fulfilled at the second coming of Christ. Then there will be Divine judgment on the nations followed by the supremacy of Israel in the Millennial Kingdom.

The immigration of Jews to their ancient homeland has earned the attention of the entire world, as well as students of biblical prophecy. This ingathering known among the Jewish people as (aliya), has populated a young nation with the cross-section of humankind needed to build, plant, harvest, educate, and even defend themselves from the surrounding nations that are determined to destroy a regathered Israel. The most exciting, documented evidence that the Lord's return could be close at hand is the activity surrounding preparations for the rebuilding of the temple-on-Temple Mount in Jerusalem. There are Jewish men who now believe they are qualified to serve as priests. Their priestly garments are made and in storage: all the implements to be used for the sacrifices and worship at the temple are ready; biblical harps are being handmade for the Levite orchestra; and a red heifer is even available for the purification of everything for the temple.

Ezekiel 40 to 46 gives detailed instructions for the temple that will stand on the Temple Mount during the Millennium. However, Daniel 9:27 states that an earlier temple, preparations for which are in process will exist in Jerusalem during the Tribulation period.

These four major areas trends-the aliya (return) of the Jewish people. The alignment of the nations, anticipation for peace, and arrangements for the temple-were actually mentioned by the ancient Jewish prophets up to 2,500 years ago. These are the signposts along the way that the prophets and Jesus alerted the Jewish people to anticipate the time of the end, the time of the second coming of Jesus Christ. Since Christ's return takes place only seven years after the Rapture, how close must the Rapture be? 22.

I will return to the subject of dreams again when discussing an Israel visit. A more recent dream was the *circumstance* of both Monique and I being attacked by evil spirits. This did not last long before the Holy Spirit rescued both of us as we were charged to rescue others who were not saved yet and lead them to Christ.

I was really humbled by the dream I had of Christ on the cross with symbolism that is somewhat difficult to explain. I was asked in the dream, what is the distance between the apex of the plus sign to the apex of the letter L? In fact, I needed to quarry a dear friend, Dr. Wood for his explanation and interpretation.

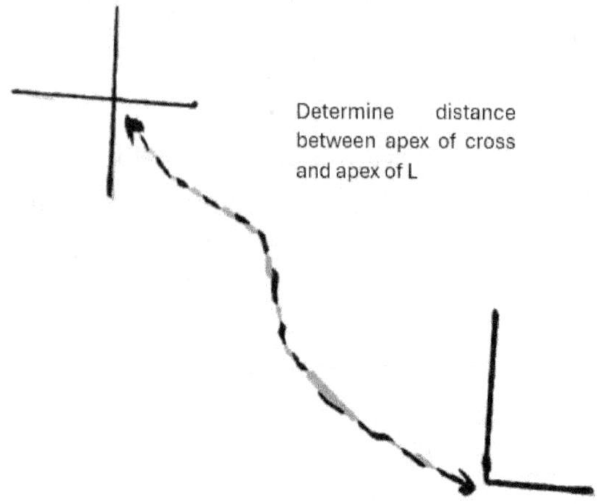

Distance?

This is how google had to describe the L. This letter is the tallest letter of the Hebrew alphabet. It represents royalty. In fact, it represents the King of all kings, the Almighty. It also represents the (lev) heart, as it is the center of the Hebrew alphabet. I pondered this for some time. Why my God was placing this in a dream for me to understand? My initial humble approach was to use math to determine the distance between the apex of the plus sign and the apex of the L. Perhaps God was simply testing me for my research. However, it did me good to find I was perhaps rather worthy of research and finding the answer. All my life I have known what Christ had done on the cross for the remission of my sins and now what a novel way (in a dream) to show me complete understanding.

Another dream I had was my placement in the clouds. These are clouds above, not a foggy day with feet planted on the ground. I was actually suspended in the air above the clouds, viewing nothing but clouds when two adults dressed as Biblical beings began passing before me, maybe ten to fifteen paces away. I could not discern who they were for their head covering was that of ancient days. Their conversation was soft, more like a murmur so I could not discern a particular language. Again, in this dream, I am positively humbled by the *circumstances*. Was I witnessing a future event to be? Was this a foretaste of being taken away as the Rapture is foretold by the Apostle Paul in 1 Thessalonians 1:17. The rapture is an eschatological position held by many Christians, particularly those of American evangelicalism, consisting of an end-time event when all Christian believers who are alive, along with resurrected believers, will rise "in the clouds, to meet the Lord in the air." "Behold, He cometh with the clouds." Revelation 1:7. It is by the very clouds that the Spirit of God is teaching us how to walk by faith. If there were no clouds, we should have no faith. "The clouds are but the dust of our Father's feet."

The clouds are a sign that He is there. What a revelation it is to know that sorrow, bereavement, and suffering are the clouds that come along with God. God cannot come near without clouds. His purpose in the cloud is to simplify our belief until our relationship with Him is exactly that of a child. Is there anyone "save Jesus only" in your cloud? "We must get to the place where there is "no one anymore, save Jesus only in our cloud." 23

This dream was logged in my journal on July 9, 2009. I was in a gathering of people like a church cell group, and I began reading scripture. I did not remember what scripture it was, only that it was in the present active tense. I did not even finish but one or two sentences it seemed, when the action of His word came into being. In other words, what was read was taking place. I stopped reading in utter awe of what had occurred. Those around me were amazed as well by the *circumstance* and stuttered, "Read on, read more." It was then that the dream ended. I thought at the time, that was really a big wow Lord Jesus.

I should mention that not all my dreams were of a spiritual nature. I still have dreams of combat both as an Infantry Officer on one tour and as a Reconnaissance Pilot on another in Vietnam. They are stressful but I awaken from them resolved that Christ Jesus in my protector, my shield, and my deliverer through all the torment and evil that may abound. Post-Traumatic Stress Disorder (PTSD) is not a good thing to live with. However, it does give me a better understanding of warfare in the Bible and how men dealt with it by drawing them closer to Almighty God. One of the better examples is King David's experience in Psalms he had written for deliverance.

DECISION AMERICA TOUR

And you shall remember that the Lord your God led you all the way these forty years in the wilderness, to humble you and test you (circumstance) to know what was in your heart, whether you would keep His commandments or not. So, He humbled you, allowed you to hunger, and fed you with manna which you did not know nor did your fathers know that He might make you know that man shall not live by bread alone; but man lives by every word that proceeds from the mouth of the Lord.

Deuteronomy 8:2-3 NIV

It was 2005 when Monique and I went on a tour of Israel which was very memorable for a couple of reasons: *circumstances*. The tour bus was traveling down the highway from Galilee toward Jerusalem. It was nearing sundown and as we were traveling up to Jerusalem. The sunset was shining on the mountains giving the appearance as if they were of gold. Monique and I were in the front seats and I noted to Monique "look, look the hills, the mountains appear as if they are of gold." I began tearing, and weeping as the guide placed this audio on the sound system.

The Holy City
Song by The Tabernacle Choir at Temple Square
Last night I lay asleeping
There came a dream so fair
I stood in old Jerusalem
Beside the temple there
I heard the children singing
And ever as they sang
Methought the voice of Angels
From Heaven in answer rang
"Jerusalem, Jerusalem!
Lift up you gates and sing
Hosanna in the highest
Hosanna to your King!"
And then methought my dream was chang'd
The streets no longer rang
Hush'd were the glad Hosannas
The little children sang
The sun grew dark with mystery
The morn was cold and chill
As the shadow of a cross arose
Upon a lonely hill
"Jerusalem, Jerusalem!
Hark! How the Angels sing
Hosanna in the highest
Hosanna to your King!"
And once again the scene was chang'd
New earth there seem'd to be
I saw the Holy City
Beside the tideless sea
The light of God was on its streets

The gates were open wide
And all who would might enter
And no one was denied
No need of moon or stars by night
Or sun to shine by day
It was the new Jerusalem
That would not pass away
"Jerusalem! Jerusalem
Sing for the night is o'er
Hosanna in the highest
Hosanna for evermore

I do not remember how many minutes the view of the setting sun remained on the hills before the sight of Jerusalem came into sight, but it was gold in appearance as well. Then as the lyrics closed, dusk was replacing the scene, but the busload of sightseers had the *circumstance* to witness the beauty of Jerusalem to come. On my second tour to Israel, I made sure I would find a copy of that Disk to play when the mood saw fit. I also searched for a painting that might capture the same scene from the West looking East but to no avail. I did find one looking West though, but not as good as I remembered.

Another event or *circumstance* that occurred during our tour of Israel that may not seem like a sign to the busload was when we pulled into a parking area beside the highway while heading South. Some might consider it just a rest stop, however, I took what the guide had to say as very important. You see, the guide was an Israeli veteran who had fought in the 1967 war that Israel was involved in. This was with five of her neighboring Arab countries. Against heavy attacking forces, not only was Israel surviving but winning. Our guide described how his unit was attacking the Gollan heights of Jordan and Syria and what they found when cresting the mountains was that the defending

Arab forces had left their fortified positions and retreated leaving weapons, ammunition, and rations without a battle. Our guide explained that the enemy had heard that the Israelis were behind them and threatening to overwhelm them. My thoughts were amazed by the manner in which God in his mercy and providence was still in modern times protecting his people.

Reference 2 Kings 7:3-20 Now there were four men who were lepers at the entrance to the gate. And they said to one another, "Why are we sitting here until we die? If we say, 'Let us enter the city,' the famine is in the city, and we shall die there. Now, therefore, come, let us surrender to the army of the Syrians. If they keep us alive, we shall live; and if they kill us, we shall only die. They rose at twilight to go to the camp of the Syrians, and when they came to the outskirts of the Syrian damp to their surprise no one was there. For the Lord had caused the army of the Syrians to hear the noise of chariots and the noise of horses-the noise of a great army so they said to one another, "Look, the king of Israel has hired against us the kings of Hittites and the kings of the Egyptians to attack us." Therefore, they arose and fled at twilight, and left the camp intact—their tents, their horses, and their donkeys – and they fled for their lives.

In the modern-day battle of 1967, Israel lost in the neighborhood of 40 tanks, whereas the combined armies of the enemy lost over 400. Israel is blessed by the hand of God and His providence. It is my belief that as a friend of Israel, America has been blessed and still is to this day.

As Celebrate Jesus missions were winding down, I was selected as a team member on the Franklin Graham Decision America Tour in Florida commencing in 2015. Pastor Jim Brissey, Senior Pastor, Higher Ground Ministries, Deland, headed up our Florida group of enthused men and women in Christ. I submit this blog: 24.

Franklin was. Not endorsing any candidate. The purpose of the prayer rallies was to motivate people to get the facts about the candidates and make a godly decision.

Franklin Graham encouraged people to prayerfully read through the pages that defined the **Democratic and Republican platforms**. Reading this information would guide your decisions on whom to cast your vote. Your vote counts. Take others to their voting stations to vote. Share your beliefs with people around you so they realize this may be the most crucial election of this century. In recent times it has been reported that Christians had not voted and as a result lost their religious way.

Prayer

Lord God Almighty, I believe you are above all kings and presidents. No one is allowed to take office without your consent. You have sent leaders to guide the nation of Israel with peace and prosperity. Other times, leaders were placed as a punishment for the sins of the people. Lord, I ask for You to forgive the sins of the United States against You. Please send godly leadership to preserve and lead the United States to a position of prominence in the world to back Israel. Please remove the "party scales" from the eyes of people which blind them to the truth for a better life. Reveal, confuse, and destroy the plans of the enemy which schemes to destroy the United States from within our borders. Please guide us to elect leaders who will promote racial unity, and peace in our communities, stop crime, increase jobs, and promote productive lifestyles. Thank you for hearing our prayer for the United States of America. We need You more now than at any time in history. Jesus, you are welcome in our communities, in Iowa, Florida, and across the United States. Thank you for unifying our people.

Thank you, Jesus. Amen.

If My people, who are called by My name,

shall humble themselves, pray, seek, crave,

And require of necessity My face and

Turn from their wicked ways,

Then will I hear from heaven,

Forgive their sin, and heal their land.

2 Chronicles 7:14 AM

o   Franklin Graham talks to a packed crowd of more than 2,500 people at the first stop of the Decision America Tour in Des Moines, Iowa, on Tuesday, Jan. 5.

Franklin Graham looks over the crowd on Tuesday on a 32-degree day in Des Moines, Iowa.

Franklin Graham walks down the steps at the Iowa Capitol.

A chilly day couldn't keep this veteran from joining the rally.

Cramming into any spot they could to catch a message of hope for our country.

More than 2,500 people turned out for the Jan. 5 Decision America stop in Iowa.

Praying for the healing of our nation. "God heard the prayer of Nehemiah and gave him a favor," Franklin Graham said.

Franklin Graham talked about when his father, Billy Graham,

was in school and how each day began with the Lord's Prayer and the Pledge of Allegiance.

Those making a pledge to God and country could text in their support.

Standing up for biblical values is one of the core tenets of the Decision America Tour.

"We need a revival among Christians to stand for our values and our beliefs," one attendee said.

Prayer groups spontaneously formed around the snowy Des Moines, Iowa Capitol.

"The moral and political walls of our nation are crumbling," Franklin Graham told the Iowa crowd.

"The most important thing we can do as Christians is pray," Franklin Graham said in Des Moines.

Tuesday's prayer rally included a time for those in attendance to confess their sins to God.

Showing their support for biblical values on Tuesday.

Dennis Agajanian warmed the crowd up and closed with an old favorite, "Nothing but the Blood."

Praising God during a time of worship in Des Moines, Iowa. One down, 49 to go. Next stop: Tallahassee, Florida.

Decision America Tour in Florida commencing in 2016. I submit this blog:

'PHENOMENAL' START TO DECISION AMERICA TOUR

by Trevor Freeze, the Billy Graham Evangelistic Association

Praising God during a time of worship in Des Moines, Iowa. One down, 49 to go. Next stop: Tallahassee, Florida.

There may not be one singular reason why more than 2,500 people would brave 30-degree weather in early January, navigating snow banks and icy steps to gather at the Des Moines, Iowa, Capitol building.

But concerned Iowan Sherri Street summed it up quite nicely.

"We can't stay the silent majority any longer."

And just like that, the Decision America Tour has left the station. Next stop: the remaining 49 state capitals.

And that *we* that Street's referring to?

It's a mass of Bible-believing Christians throughout the United States of America, who have seen their country stray far from its beginnings—or even just a few generations ago, when Billy Graham began his school days with a recitation of the Lord's Prayer and Pledge of Allegiance.

And those Ten Commandments that once hung on the wall? Nobody even wonders what closet those ended up in.

"Our country is in trouble," Franklin Graham, president of the Billy Graham Evangelistic Association, began the prayer rally. "It's in big-time trouble. The moral and political walls of our nation are crumbling.

"The most important thing we can do as Christians is pray."

After a time of worship music and prayer and 30 minutes of Franklin Graham sharing his heart for this country, his ending was similar, but with a significant and optimistic tone of returning to "one nation under God."

Franklin Graham shares his heart for America with Des Moines, Iowa.

Judy Winegan, who came to the prayer rally with her friend Street, was moved to tears talking about the rally afterward.

"It was phenomenal," she said, collecting her words. "I think if America doesn't change, America will fall."

"It needs to be said," Street talked about Franklin Graham's message.

"And it needs to be prayed," Winegan added.

Among the 2,500-plus on Tuesday was one man who drove 12 hours from Sevierville, Tennessee. Morgan Austin, 44, drove his wife and three young children four hours from Lincoln, Nebraska, only to hop back in the minivan and return straight home.

"I think (Franklin Graham) is awesome," Austin said. "He's the one person in America who has the respect to do this. He's the singular voice right now.

"We prayed for him last night."

The oldest Austin child, Jordan, 10, brought home more than just an America flag: "It was so good, it made me cry," he said.

The message was straight-forward but included something for everyone. It started with a call to pray and repent.

Jumping off from the story of Nehemiah rebuilding the walls of Jerusalem, Franklin Graham offered opportunities for people to confess sins—of their nation, their own, and their fathers.

"God heard the prayer of Nehemiah and gave him a favor," he told the crowd.

Franklin Graham also gave a clear Gospel message and an opportunity for anyone in attendance to accept Christ and respond via text message for follow-up materials.

"If you don't remember anything else," he said. "Remember this —God loves you."

Prior to Iowa and the balance of 49 states there were years of planning and preparation. One of the items in the sack full of material was a DVD entitled "Value of a Soul" recording the life of three people who came to Christ. These stories were wonderfully choreographed of actual events. One story was that of a soldier in Afghanistan who had lost his eyesight from an enemy explosion of his vehicle. Through his recovery, he came to Christ Jesus and trained for the "Iron Man" competition. He obviously had to be tethered to another individual in this exhausting series of events. He did not win the competition, but he finished the events to the glory of God. What a testimony to share with one who may not believe. Then, it is our turn in Tallahassee, FL.

"I've got a question for you," Franklin Graham asked the crowd. "Are your sins forgiven?"

A patriotic moment at Tuesday's prayer rally.

Franklin Graham shared about his father, Billy Graham, who went to school at a time when the Pledge of Allegiance was recited every day, along with the Lord's Prayer.

The Tommy Coomes Band encouraged the crowd with their song, "My Hope."

Those who wanted to make a commitment to both God and America were asked to take out their smartphones and text in their pledges.

"I pray that God would hear our prayers today and give us a favor," Franklin Graham told the crowd in Tallahassee, Florida.

"Let's take this nation back!" Franklin Graham said as he concluded the Florida prayer rally on Tuesday.

The Decision America Sunshine State Tour is the second Decision America Tour to take place in the state. The first prayer event with Franklin Graham was held at the Capitol in Tallahassee in 2016.

A 'Monumental' Finish to the Decision America Tour

By **Trevor Freeze** • *October 13, 2016*

A crowd estimated to be more than 14,000 strong joined Franklin Graham in Raleigh, North Carolina, for the 50th and final Decision America Tour prayer rally on Thursday, Oct. 13, 2016.

An outdoor event in Iowa. During the middle of a workday. In January.

Franklin Graham had a unique calling: to hold prayer rallies in all 50 state capitals. But he'll be the first to tell you that 282 days ago, waiting for noon to come around in windy and snowy Des Moines, with temperatures in the teens—it was a bit of a challenge.

"I thought to myself, if 50 people showed up, that would be a pretty good crowd," Franklin Graham said, opening the final Decision America Tour stop on Thursday in Raleigh, North Carolina.

Fifty? Ha.

An estimated 2,500 concerned Americans launched Franklin Graham's "campaign for God" that day in January on the ice-packed Iowa State Capitol steps. The Decision America Tour was officially off and running.

Finishing the tour with a massive crowd of about 14,200 in his home state, he reflected on when it all began.

"They didn't come to hear me," Franklin Graham said. "They came to pray."

Did they ever? Attendees endured 18-degree bitterness in Concord, New Hampshire; downpours in Jefferson City, Missouri; a 100-degree heat index in Springfield, Illinois.

Protesters tried to derail the tour—particularly organizers in California, Wisconsin, and in the upper corners of the U.S. But nothing stopped nearly a quarter of a million people from standing with Franklin Graham across the nation, passionately crying out to God to save this country.

And nothing has changed the message.

"America is in trouble," Franklin Graham said on the steps of the North Carolina State Capitol Thursday. "Our only hope is in Almighty God."

Rapid Response Team chaplains join in prayer during the final stop of the Decision America Tour.

A total of 236,950—an average of nearly 5,000 people per stop—joined the Decision America Tour in person. Add to that, there were more than 150,000 live views online. That Thursday alone, over 287,000 people watched via Facebook Live. Franklin Graham's three-fold message was simple and study: Pray. Vote. Engage.

"Freedom of religion was intended so we can live out our religion 24/7," Franklin Graham said. "Our job as Christians is to make the impact of Christ felt in every facet of life."

Among the 14,000-plus crowd on Thursday were Diane and Randy Vaughn, who drove 90 miles from Kernersville, North Carolina, to witness the historic tour finale.

"I agree with everything Franklin Graham said, period," Randy said. "I think it's monumental," Diane said of the tour's final stop. "He's a bold voice. Everyone knows the Graham name. And to go to every state capital shows his commitment and his service to the Lord. I don't know anyone else who has done this.

"I think it's pretty cool that he did stop Number 50 here in North Carolina."

More than 111,000 people have signed the Decision America Tour pledge, which calls on Christians to live out their faith in private and public, vote for candidates who support biblical values, and prayerfully consider running for office.

In other words: Pray. Vote. Engage.

"I was just talking to my husband about running for an office," Raleigh resident Lynn Dixon said. "I don't know what office, but I'm going to start praying about it. Franklin said start praying about running, and I can do that."

In addition to calling Christians to action, Franklin Graham has shared a clear Gospel message at all 50 stops, giving everyone in attendance an opportunity to make a decision to follow Jesus Christ. As a result, more than 8,000 people nationwide had responded. "If you've never invited Christ in your heart, you can do that right now," he said on that Thursday.

The tour ended with Franklin Graham imploring everyone to keep praying for America, to get involved in local politics, and to be a "community organizer for God."

Just before the final shofar was blown, he reminded those listening of the difference they could make.

"We can only do it if we surrender ourselves completely to God, allowing Him to work in us," Franklin Graham said. "We need your voice. We need the Christian voice."

Fired-up and ready to act, Dixon added a hearty amen to what was said on Thursday.

"Oh, my goodness, we've got to pray," she said. "I know Franklin Graham is a praying man. I know God had to call him to do this.

"I just hope God calls him to do some more."

My humble participation in Decision America was at times a feverous pace of meetings, exhortation, and prayer. It was, however, one of the most rewarding endeavors of my life. Some of the material provided then, I still use today like the DVD, "Value of a Soul."

When you are involved with the depth and width of prayer throughout the land you become more aware of His presence and are strangely warmed in losing track of time. The Decision America Tour was not the only group of people and churches praying for the election of 2016. You find out in other lands especially Israel that our land was being was being globally prayed for regarding the outcome. And what we ended up with was an unlikely candidate who won. Yet, he became one of the most hated presidents by a segment of the population. What is very important, however, this president chose to recognize Jerusalem as Israel's capital. These circumstances overwhelming point to a God who through unlikely events brings about His providence. Trump recognized Jerusalem as Israel's Capital and ordered the U.S. Embassy to move to Jerusalem.

The president cast his decision as a break with decades of failed policy on Jerusalem, which the United States, along with virtually every other nation in the world, has declined to recognize as the capital since Israel's founding in 1948. That policy, he said, brought us "no closer to a lasting peace agreement between Israel and the Palestinians."

Mr. Trump's remarks were the most closely scrutinized of his presidency on the Middle East, where he has vowed to broker the "ultimate deal" between Israelis and Palestinians but has yet to find a breakthrough to end the conflict. He said he remained committed to brokering an agreement "that is a great deal for the Israelis and a great deal for the Palestinians."

The president said the decision to recognize Jerusalem should not be construed as the United States taking a position on whether, or how, the city might ultimately be shared. But he offered little solace to the Palestinians, making no mention of their long-held hopes for East Jerusalem to be the capital of a Palestinian state.

Instead, Mr. Trump emphasized the domestic political dimension of the decision. He noted that he had promised to move the embassy during the 2016 presidential campaign, and added, "While previous presidents have made this a major campaign promise, they failed to deliver. Today, I am delivering."

Though he did not mention it, Mr. Trump signed the same national security waiver signed by his predecessors, from Barack Obama to George W. Bush to Bill Clinton, which will allow the administration to keep the embassy in Tel Aviv for an additional six months. White House officials said that was unavoidable because it would take several years to move the embassy staff to a new facility in Jerusalem.

There was, of course, disagreement and dissent regarding that announcement, but he appealed for calm, moderation, and for the voices of tolerance to prevail over the purveyors of hate.

Mr. Trump's promise to move the embassy appealed to evangelical voters and pro-Israel American Jews. By delivering on that promise, Mr. Trump's aides said, he was enhancing his credibility as a peacemaker.

The announcement, officials said at the time, was a recognition of current and historic reality. West Jerusalem is the seat of Israel's government and recognizing it as such would remove ambiguity from the American position up to that timeframe.

Jerusalem was and is still today, one of the world's most fiercely contested swaths of real estate, with each side disputing the other's claims. Palestinians view East Jerusalem as the capital of a future Palestinian state, and most of the world considers it occupied territory. Jerusalem's Old City has the third-holiest mosque in Islam and the holiest site in Judaism, making the city's status a sensitive issue for Muslims and Jews alike. Jerusalem is also sacred ground to Christians.

In addition to declining to take a position on the ultimate shape of Jerusalem, Mr. Trump called for the status quo on a disputed area of the Old City, known as the Temple Mount to Jews and the Noble Sanctuary to Muslims, which has been a flash point for tensions. 26.

One may ask, why is Jerusalem so important to be completely in the hands of Israel? For Bible-believing people, Jerusalem is the city that Christ Jesus returns to after the tribulation.

... the joy of the whole earth... Mount Zion, the city of the Great King.

Psalms 48:1-2

Christians do well to pay attention to what is happening in Jerusalem, not because it is a shrine and not because it is more important than the New Jerusalem that is to come. Jerusalem is a timeclock for events of the last days.

Also of note is that Jerusalem is one of the elements of the "Apple of God's eye" Lam 2:18 (NKJ) Their heart cried unto the Lord...daughter of Zion...let not the apple of thine eye cease. (Jerusalem)

Read Jerusalem in the last days in Luke 21:5-16

Jesus ascended to heaven from the Mount of Olives, on the east side of Jerusalem, and Jesus is coming again to the same place. [Acts 1:9-12 *and* Zechariah 14:4-5]

WITNESSING CHRIST JESUS

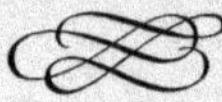

Romans 8:37-39. Yet in all these things we are more than conquerors through Him who loved us. For I am persuaded that neither death nor life, nor angels nor principalities nor powers, nor things present nor things to come, nor height nor depth, nor any other created thing, shall be able to separate us from the love of God which is in Christ Jesus our Lord.

Romans 8:27 NIV

The *circumstances* here describe a situation of profound magnificent providence. All one nonbeliever needs to do is understand and humbly accept Christ as in Romans 10:9. "That if you shall confess with your mouth the Lord Jesus and shall believe in your heart that God has raised him from the dead, you shall be saved." There is no mystery here. The difficulty with many, however, is how do you find out who is or is not saved without interacting with them verbally. The point is that we believers must engage people.

When Monique and I moved to Texas in 2016 I was searching for a venue that would allow me to witness. I began in a coffee shop sipping coffee as I talked with different people. I got this idea from a mission where a retired pastor would set up a card table and two folding chairs in a covered walkway in front of several stores (small strip malls). One of the businesses was a wash-a-tera. His worn Bible was in plain sight on the table. As patrons had loads of washing in process the pastor would witness to them if they chose to visit with him and talk. In like manner, I chose a coffee shop that allowed me to sit and witness those at my table or other tables as I moved about. I did not experience measurable success, perhaps in part due to my impatience.Wait upon the Lord is in a number of Bible passages and to this day as an octogenarian, I struggle with this issue. "But they that wait upon the Lord shall renew their strength; they shall mount up with wings as eagles; they shall run, and not be weary; and they shall walk, and not faint." (Isa 40:31.)

Another ministry that I was involved with in Florida was, "Revival Prayer Connection Tallahassee". This ministry began with the idea of three women each from a different denomination. Their connection was that they met on a Big Bend Walk to Emmaus event and thought it would be good if they got their three churches together once a month for a spiritual talk followed by groups of (four to five) for prayer time. By word of mouth and some publicity, the group of three churches grew to over thirty participating churches of many denominations. This ministry flowed very well for just over three years until from what I heard was fatigue among the number of volunteers needed to keep up with the administration and operation.

Here in the Northeast San Antonio area, I began going from church to church to inquire about their interests in establishing a Revival Prayer Connection. This was before finally settling into our current church. There was interest in the surrounding community, however, none great enough to begin.

It was during the time our grandchildren from Florida were visiting us in 2017, that while we were walking about San Antonio I grew wary. I stopped to rest at what I thought was a USO (United Services Organization) outlet. As it turned out it was actually the Christian Service Center, an independent 501c3 center supported by many churches. This visit led to an appointment for an interview followed by wonderful years of volunteer service witnessing young Airmen, Soldiers, Sailors, Marines, and Coast Guard.

Fridays and Saturdays were busy days at the center located one block from the Alamo. The reason was, it was graduation ceremonies for Air Force basic training at Lackland Air Force Base. Tradition has allowed parents of new Airmen to visit the base and see their sons and daughters parade in review. This is followed by visits to take in the various sights of San Antonio like the famous Alamo and River Walk.

The Christian Service Centers have seen the need to reach our military young people for Christ and providing for them a "Home-Away-From-Home" with the Bible. The Christian Service Center is not a church, but it complements the ministries of local churches by meeting the needs of military personnel that may not be recognized within the local church community. They have a non-denominational Statement of Faith and are an evangelistic Christian outreach to those who serve in the Armed Forces.

The men and women in uniform are offered a safe environment of recreation, relaxation, and refreshments at no cost to them. They are also able to participate in a longstanding local military tradition (in San Antonio since August 1978) where they place a pin for their hometown on the map of their state. If the military person does not stop in on their own, we volunteers go outside and invite them in for them to sign our books where they are from.

One Christian family with a mix of ethnicities placed a pin on their current U.S. address. One of the adopted children asked if she might place a pin in the African country where she was born. How warm was that situation? It was very comforting with hugs of recognition of how great our God is. Other service people find the piano and start playing Christian hymns. So, there they are in sing-alongs glorifying God.

Of course, there are the prayer rooms where we would invite the unsaved. We would lead them to Christ through scripture and prayer. Here, the Holy Spirit is involved with touching their hearts with the comfort of God's grace. It is a beautiful sight to experience with them. The parents are invited into the prayer room as well to experience seeing their child accept Christ Jesus as their Lord and Savior. The joy of this *circumstance* is often expressed in tears of happiness especially grandparents who often have a very good understanding of life in Christ.

The center has had parents accept Christ Jesus along with their military children which then becomes a multi-faceted joyful experience. In this situation (*circumstance*) after prayer, I announce to the family, "Do you know there are angels in heaven joyfully singing praise to God on High."

Time is not on the side of those serving at the center for the family has only a limited amount of time to visit San Antonio sites and get their military son or daughter back to Lackland Air Force base before 6:00 p.m. So, the peak period is between 10:00 a.m. and 3:00 p.m. Since you need to account for lunch, your time to witness becomes more hurried than you would like. However, one must be satisfied with the amount of time

God has allowed us. Even so, it is physically and spiritually exhausting with the tempo of leading one to Christ Jesus. I am reminded of the parable of the Sower found in Matthew, Mark, and Luke.

Airman with family visiting center.

After serving at the center for nearly three years, I moved on to Brook Army Medical Facility. Here, I pray for patients before surgery or with family members waiting on loved ones who may be in the Intensive Care Unit (ICU). Brooke Army Medical Center (BAMC), at Joint Base San Antonio-Fort Sam Houston, is one of the United States Military Health System's premier medical facilities employing approximately 8,500 active duty, federal civilian, and contract health care professionals who care for more than 4,000 patients each day.

Here, one could say I have slowed down or rather paced myself a bit although I still manage tithing time to the Lord in scripture and prayer. I still do not lose the opportunity to witness Christ Jesus and the cross when the opportunity presents itself in any encounter with people who may not know Him.

CIRCUMSTANCES FOR PRAYER
AND CHANGES

I make known the end from the beginning, from ancient times, what is still to come. I say, "My purpose will stand, and I will do all that I please."

Isaiah 46:10 NIV

In this scripture, God is declaring how things turn out long before they happen. God is also declaring that not just natural events but human events are not yet done.

Through peace and security or be it calamity, when we abide in Christ Jesus, He abides in us. This is addressed in John 17, Christ's prayer to His father in heaven. Christ was at home with God wherever His body was placed. He never chose His own *circumstances* but was meek towards His father's dispensation for Him. We as believers are called as well to consciously or unconsciously abide in Christ Jesus wherever we are placed.

Throughout the Bible, God used *circumstances* to lead his people and accomplish His will. Here are a few more examples:

- Joseph reveals himself – Genesis 45
- Esther was in the King's house when Mordecai "For such a time as this"- Esther 4
- End of Job's troubles and because he remained faithful – Job 42,
- God extended Hezekiah's life – Isaiah 38.
- Daniel in the lion's den – Daniel 6.

I particularly like the story of King Naaman in 2 Kings 5. Naaman was sent to Elisha, a mighty prophet of God in Israel to be supernaturally healed. Instead of Elisha coming to the door to greet Naaman, he sent a messenger to say to him, "go wash yourself in the Jordan River seven times, and your flesh will be restored to you, and you shall be clean."

Finally, King Naaman states, "Behold now I know that there is no God in all the earth, but in Israel; now therefore I pray you, take a blessing of your servant." The gift was refused for the grace of God is free to receive. The is a very fine story to use while witnessing to unbelievers.

God has a perfect will; man invented a permissive will through disobedience. In spite of man's failures, God is always trying to draw man unto Himself and lead us in the correct path.

Several years ago, while I was researching a paper, I noticed that God counted several areas as, "The Apple of His eye".

Being the apple of God's eye means being at the very center of His focus and protection. He loves and protects even when his people are stubborn and rebellious or are caught in the worst of situations. His care remains constant.

In a similar fashion, we are to keep God and His instructions as the apple of our eyes. When we are focused on Him, our own rebellion and worry melt away as we see ourselves where we truly are if we are in Christ, protected as in the apple of God's eye.

Apple of God's Eye only occurs in five verses (KJV)

1. Deu 32:10 He found him in a desert land...He instructed him...He kept him as the apple of His eye. (The Jewish People) Note: As Gentile believers, we are grafted in. Romans 11:11
2. Psa 17:8 Keep me as the apple of thine eye, hide me under the shadow of thy wing. (The King)
3. Pro 7:2 Keep my commandments, and live: and my law as the apple of thine eye (The Word)
4. Lam 2:38 Their heart cried unto the Lord...daughter of Zion...let not the apple of thine eye cease. (Jerusalem)
5. Zec 2:8 For thus saith the Lord of Host: After the glory hath he sent me unto the nations which spoiled you; for he [that] toucheth you toucheth the apple of His eye (Israel)

Before closing in prayer, I wish to make reference to a note in my Evidence Bible commentary by Ray Comfort

Ref: Colossians 1:28 Reflections on our primary task. A light-house keeper gained a reputation as being a very kind man. He would give free fuel to ships that miscalculated the amount of fuel needed to reach their destination port. One night during a storm, lightning struck his lighthouse and put out his light. He immediately turned on his generator, but it soon ran out of fuel, for he had given his reserves to passing ships. During the dark night, a ship struck the rocks, and many lives were lost.

At his trial, the judge knew of the lighthouse keeper's reputation as a kind man and wept as he gave a sentence. He accused the lighthouse keeper of neglecting his primary responsibility-to keep the light shining.

Some churches can so often get caught up in legitimate acts of kindness- standing for political righteousness, feeding the hungry, but our primary task is to warn sinners of danger. We are to keep the light of the gospel shining so that sinners can avoid the jagged-edged rocks of wrath and escape being eternally damned.

My friend, I stand in judgment now

and feel that you're to blame somehow.

On earth, I walked with you by day,

and never did you show the way.

You knew the Savior in truth and glory,

But never did you tell the story.

My knowledge then was very dim,

You could have led me safely to Him.

Though we lived together, here on earth,

You never told me of the second birth,

And now I stand before eternal hell,

because of heaven's glory you did not tell.

(Anonymous) 26.

"Each person we meet on a daily basis who does not know Christ is hell-bound. That may make some folks bristle-but it's a fact. When we refuse to warn people that their actions and lifestyles have eternal consequences, we're not doing" doing them any favors. If everybody feels good about his or her sin, why would anyone repent?" Franklin Graham. 27.

"If they are breathing...they need Jesus". Mark Cahill

(Extracted from Evidence Bible)

I often feel convicted when I witness Christ Jesus and the cross and there is no positive response, I ask myself, did I spend sufficient time with the individual? Did I not consider that more important than the task I was on at the time? After departing the situation, the Holy Spirit lets me know what I may have done or rather what I should have done. Winners of Souls must first be weepers of souls. Charles Spurgeon. The aim of all servants is to secure the realization of Jesus Christ in every set of *circumstances* he or she may be in.

There are many prayers in our Bible and I have always cherished Christ Jesus' Prayer in Gethsemane, John 17 or Daniel's prayer for his people, Daniel 9:1-19, however,

for the purpose of this book and more relevant today, I have selected a prayer taken from Chuck Missler's book on Romans. When minister Joe Wright was asked to open the new session of the Kansas State legislature, everyone was expecting the usual politically correct generalities, but what they heard instead was a stirring prayer, passionately calling our country to repentance and righteousness. (The response was immediate. A number of the Legislature walked out during the prayer in protest. In 6 short weeks, the Central Christian Church had logged more than 5,000 responding calls, with only 47 of those calls responding negatively. The church is now receiving international requests for copies of the prayer from India, Africa, and Korea.) "Heavenly Father, we come before you today and ask Your forgiveness and seek Your direction and guidance. We know Your Word says, "Woe on those who call evil good, but that's exactly what we have done. We have lost our spiritual equilibrium and reversed our values. We confess that: We have ridiculed the absolute truth of Your Word and called it pluralism. We have worshiped other gods and called it multiculturalism. We have endorsed perversion and called it an alternative lifestyle. We have exploited the poor and called it the lottery. We have neglected the needy and called it self-preservation. We have rewarded laziness and called it welfare. We have killed our unborn and called it a choice. We have shot abortionists and called it justifiable. We have neglected to discipline our children and called it building self-esteem. We have abused power and called it political savvy. We have coveted our neighbor's possessions and called it ambition. We have polluted the air with profanity and pornography and called it enlightenment.

"Search us, O God, and know our hearts today; cleanse us from every sin and set us free. Guide and bless these men and women who have been sent to direct us to the center of your will I ask it in the name of Your Son, the Living Savior, Jesus Christ, Amen.

Now, I wish to further the above prayer with "The Apple of God's Eye". Lord God almighty I pray a blessing upon Jerusalem, your beautiful holy city on a hill, now the capital of Israel yet again, however, more importantly than this, it is the city of your return Christ Jesus, after the tribulation. Lord God, I pray a blessing on Israel. Bless the peace and prosperity of Israel as well as the increase. Bless, bless, bless the Jewish people; the Hebrew people of the earth. Bless their regathering unto Israel from the four corners of the world as it is written and occurring through the ages. More importantly, bless the Hebrews/Jews turning unto Christ Jesus so that they, the remnant, along with the fullness of the gentiles come in so that we as one church, one body may celebrate the wedding feast of the Lamb. I pray Maranatha, maranatha, (our Lord come). Bless your Word O God, bless the bounty of your Word. Bless the power of Your Word. Bless creation in Your Word. Bless the truth of Your Word. Bless the wisdom of Your word. Bless the healing and wellness in Your Word, body, mind, and soul. Bless the magnificent glory of Your Word.

Bless the spread of Your Word as well as the understanding of Your Word. Bless the comfort of Your Word, particularly in times of trouble and pain. Bless, bless, bless the prayers in Your Word, prayers of worship, prayers of thanksgiving, prayers of faith, prayers of intercession. Bless and praise prayers of consecration and prayers of the Holy Spirit. Bless the love, mercy, grace, and salvation found in Your Word for all humankind so that through hearing, seeing, dreams, visions, and *circumstances* they turn unto You Christ Jesus believe, and are saved.

I pray a bountiful measure of the fruit of the Spirit upon all Judeo-Christian clergy throughout the world enabling them to more powerfully teach and proclaim the good news, Jesus is the Messiah, Jesus is Emanual, Christ Jesus is our Redeemer and Savior, Lord God Almighty. I pray a large portion of the fruit of the Holy Spirit on all U.S. Government elect at all levels of government up to and including the presidency and congress causing them to turn from their evil ways unto doing right by Your Word. Thank You, thank You, Lord Jesus, Amen.

NOTES

1. Source: "The Way We Really Were," by Douglas Miller and Marion Novak.
2. The Back to God Hour was a 30-minute radio program that explored a Christian perspective on faith and life.
3. Orange City Tulip Festival 2007 promotional pamphlet pictures
4. Extract, googled history of Poitiers
5. Gap between H.S. and college, Economic Studies, Brookings Institute
6. Assassination of John F. Kennedy - Wikipedia Uncategorized by David O'Brien
7. Shock of losing our President
8. Return to the Military as a Lieutenant
9. 3rd Battalion, 8th Infantry, 1st Brigade After Action Report, Battle of Three Trees, Vietnam 1967
10. Book, The War of Innocents by Bracelen Flood
11. After the Action Report of the Battle of Three Trees
12. God is our shield, Devotional by Oswald Chambers
13. The two Vietnams (1954-1965) Wikipedia
14. Just Cause War Theory by Saint Augustine. The morality of war from a Christian perspective
15. Extract, The 1973 Paris Peace Accords ending Vietnam War
16. My Utmost for His Highest, Oswald Chambers devotional
17. Book: Did You Know Thierry
18. History of Celebrate Jesus (CJ) missions
19. Pew Research September 2021
20. Franklin Graham Festival 2001

21. 2004 Extract from Dr Eric Hallett's doctoral Dissertation
22. Source: Commentary, Israel Today by Jimmy DeYoung, Tim LaHaye Prophecy Study Bible.
23. Devotional, His Utmost for His Highest by Oswald Chambers
24. Franklin Graham Decision America Tour 2015-2016
25. Reference, Mark Landler, New York Times, Dec 6, 2017
26. LaHaye Prophecy Bible
27. Franklin Graham Decision America Tour
28. Mark Cahill's Evidence Bible
29. Chuck Miller's Book on Romans

ADDENDUM

KEY BRIDGE HAS FALLEN

I came to the conclusion that week after the Key Bridge was struck March 26 and fell that there was a connection between this event and a vote by the UN Security Council demanding an immediate Gaza ceasefire on March 25. In the past, if it had not been in Israel's favor, the U.S. would veto the adverse measure. In this case, the U.S. abstained allowing the measure to pass.

The measure may have sounded good, but it was condemning Israel's further war on evil Hamas fighters which I believe to be justified. Note: "Just Cause" warfare. I believe it was also within the Providence of our God which was demonstrated by the striking of the Key Bridge named after the author of our National Anthem. This occurred the following day of the UN vote. Was not this occurrence, circumstance, a way God was warning the U.S. to return unto Him and support the Apple of His Eye, Israel?

We are living in the end of END TIMES and I wonder just how many more signs we will encounter before God deems that it is enough.

In Christ,

Bro Gene Kobes